FILL
YOURSELF
Bloom

A MOTHER'S PATH
TO UNFOLDING

Helping women learn how to unfold,
expand, and bloom to maintain their
identity alongside motherhood

By

Jennifer Banks

LET YOURSELF *Bloom*

Copyright © 2024 by Jennifer Banks

Hardcover ISBN: 978-1-961098-64-0
Paperback ISBN: 978-1-961098-63-3
eBook ISBN: 978-1-961098-65-7
Printed in the USA.

Joan of Arc Publishing
Meridian, ID 83646
www.joapublishing.com

TABLE OF
CONTENTS

PROLOGUE

Nobody told me I could choose to be anything other than a mother. I carried around the expectation in my heart that the peak of my life would be motherhood. When I was eleven years old, the first "job" I took on in society was babysitting. Later, I was enrolled in the required family science and consumer science classes at school to prepare to be a domestic goddess. I had countless religious lessons on the importance of the highest calling of *mother*.

Mother figures were everywhere I went, and I had a front row seat to the highlight reel of motherhood. Mothers bonding effortlessly with their babies through nursing, sticky smiles after cooking with mom in the kitchen, cozy cuddles, and reading on the couch with mom. Happy families on outings together, colorful drawings displayed on fridges and walls, lots of laughter, celebrations of "firsts," and the joy of always having little buddies around.

I was conditioned to want to be a mother, and the conditioning worked. As soon as I was engaged to be married, the conversations about the timing of parenthood began. We decided to give ourselves two years to be a couple before trying to get pregnant. After those first two years, it took nearly one year to get pregnant with my oldest child. It was time to have a baby, now where was it? *I was filled with longing.*

I had no idea while I was experiencing this that it would *only* take a year to get pregnant. To me it felt like it was going to be my *entire life*—a life I had no idea what to do with because children were my end goal. I tried to talk myself out of the hurt: "People struggle for years, decades, a lifetime with infertility and you can't even handle a few months?" I had to avoid social media because I couldn't stand seeing posts about stroller recommendations, playdates at the park, or gender reveals.

The following quote really resonated for me and validated my suffering:

> "There will always be someone who has an objectively harder life. There will always be someone suffering in ways you never have to think about. This doesn't mean you aren't allowed to grieve your circumstances. No one says you don't deserve to feel joy or gratitude because there are people who have it better than you. Similarly, it doesn't make sense to discount your struggles just because things could be worse off."[1]
> **—Daniell Koepke**

I was raised to think that my circumstances weren't "bad enough" to justify complaints. When I would bring up pain or heartache, I was often given examples of pioneers or people with incurable diseases to compare my own experience to. There has since been a strong movement of people learning how to feel their emotions as well as

---

[1] Instagram story from Daniell Koepke (@unapolgetically.humann) and shared here with permission from Daniell.

engaging in gentle parenting or re-parenting. Yes, people have had it worse, but that doesn't negate our own suffering.

It took a long time for my pregnancy to truly sink in. I was in denial that, after waiting and praying for so long, this desirable expectation was really coming to fruition. I had a very easy nine months of pregnancy and a very long labor and delivery (thirty-four hours that resulted in a C-section).

When I was single, everyone wanted to know when I was getting married. After I got married, everyone wanted to know when I was having children. Once I had a child, everyone wanted to know when I was going to have another. In retrospect, I am grateful for the time it took to get pregnant because it caused me to examine myself. Who was I going to show up as, whether I had children or not?

Our growth does not end when we become mothers; it continues. Of course we grow within motherhood, but we don't need to discount or ignore the growth in other areas of our identity as well. We are so conditioned to want children. For some it is religious, for others it is cultural. I hopped on the bandwagon because it seemed like the natural next step. But what about the process of *becoming* a mother? How do we assimilate this new identity into the person we are?

Do you feel like motherhood just happened to you? Did you choose to become a mom? Nobody comes up to us and asks, "Have you decided whether or not you're going to be a mom?" No, no. They ask "when?" When are you going to have children? When are you going to have more? Just because there's a door, that doesn't mean we have to open it. But if you do, own the choice to walk through it. Choose your hard. Choose to have children, and then choose again to keep them.

I'm embarrassed to tell you this, but in the early stages of motherhood, I didn't love my life. I struggled with the process of matrescence (transitioning into motherhood). Leading up to motherhood, I was accustomed to being highly productive, ambitious, and I often based my worth on my achievements. Now, suddenly, I had a child taking all of my time and energy. My days looked much different than they used to and I felt my worth and identity start to slip away. I let myself be consumed with motherhood and leaned into this new role.

This new role involved having sore nipples, being pooped on, and experiencing postpartum depression. Because of the highlight reel I'd associated with motherhood, I wasn't prepared for the effort shock of around-the-clock care, an infant needing me constantly, the loneliness and isolation, all the crying (from myself and my baby), and the high demand of new expectations placed upon me as a mother. I experienced expectation pain as I reconciled the life I thought I would have and the life I was currently living.

Three years into mothering, I heard a mom on a podcast say, "I love my children, but I don't love motherhood." Wait, what? Can we say that out loud? This mom was speaking her mind, owning the truth that motherhood isn't always a thing to cherish, desire, and behold. I had put all of my eggs into the basket of motherhood and thought I was stuck with the basket. This statement provided new hope, new possibilities, new permission to love other things besides motherhood.

Why does this feel embarrassing? Why is it unconventional to state these things? Why is it not okay to say that motherhood is not what we wanted? The guidebook to motherhood was handed down from my ancestors. And it did not make sense to me. It's as if it was filled with unfamiliar formulas or written in a different language.

From the beginning of time, people lived in groups to have a better chance at survival. Women weren't as emotionally concerned about their identity because they were concerned about food, shelter, and protection from enemies. In a smaller social group, women would fall more naturally into the identities that best showcased their talents and benefited their communities. In an ever-growing urban atmosphere, and with an increase in relationships abroad and online, women are more isolated in their motherhood duties and individual identities than ever before.

Have you found yourself having any of these thoughts?

> I don't want to do "just this" every day.
> I don't want to "only" be a mom.
> I just want to be a working mom.
> My husband makes enough money to support us, but
> I want to work outside the home.
> Who am I beyond motherhood?

This book is for women who are ready to reclaim their identity. It's for the women who don't always fit the mom stereotype: the ones who aren't happily painting every day alongside their child, the ones who don't feel connected to themselves, the ones who are envious of people who are pursuing their own interests, the ones who want to enjoy motherhood but don't fit into the mold. This is for you because it's my story of matrescence and adjusting to a new normal of life in the "fifth trimester," and there were no books for me to read about these feelings of being stuck in motherhood.

Motherhood is akin to flowers blooming in a garden: they don't just appear one day. There's an actual process from how they germinate to how they blossom. Similarly, we don't just show up with our potential fulfilled . . . we have to bloom. This book is here to help you bloom.

Before you set out to plant a garden, there is a planning and preparation phase. You have to decide what you're planting and when. In a cut-flower garden, the goal is to harvest bouquets. We're going to compare ourselves to flower bouquets composed of many "identity" flowers—sown seeds that have been intentionally cultivated to maturity. This planning and preparation can take place before you even step foot in your garden. Some gardeners enjoy sketching out a vision of their garden on paper prior to setting foot on the soil.

When I was pregnant with my oldest child, motherhood suddenly became especially relevant. What I saw and heard women talk about was how they'd lost their identity during motherhood. Once their children grew or left the house, they no longer knew what to do with themselves. They hadn't been as active in pursuing their personal hobbies and interests as they had in helping their children pursue *their* dreams and talents—motherhood was practically their only identity flower.

I carried this awareness into my journey as a mother. I started with a deliberate intention to cultivate all aspects of my identity while also nurturing my children in my role of motherhood. This perspective shapes how I approach mothering.

You might be late in the growing season, and that's okay. Be intentional as you finish out this period of your life. Then, make a plan to bloom next growing season. How do you know when that is? It depends on which seeds you sow. Consider which ones will grow best in your current environment. I'm inviting you to trust me in this growing process. Take the ideas that resonate and plant them. Leave the rest.

If you are a mother, motherhood will become just one of the many flowers in your bouquet—a part of your diverse identity. Throughout this book, you'll discover how to choose your seeds, nurture your flowers and then maintain their vitality while also fostering the growth of other goals. You'll learn to recognize when adjustments are needed, understand the importance of challenging periods, and embrace opportunities for new growth. As the curator of your life, you'll support your own growth empowered, liberated, and knowing you deserve to be nurtured and loved.

There is a lot of symbolism I will walk you through in this book. Section 1 focuses on allowing growth. You will learn how to plant and nurture the seeds in your garden. Before you can plant your seeds, however, you'll need to test your soil; this will ensure that the ground is conducive to growth. You will also learn about the importance of consistent watering and how to curate your garden to your preferences.

If you're aware of areas that may be deficient and you make changes to correct that, then you will be more likely to succeed in growing a full, sensational bouquet.

Section 2 hones in on specific considerations within your unique garden. You will learn how to balance the demands of life while also pursuing your own passions. Eradicating weeds will make for a more spacious garden. You will also discover the importance of "wintering" experiences as they relate to seed germination.

Lastly, in Section 3, you will learn how to completely unfold and bloom in your highest power, encompassed in a community of support. You will put all of your cut flowers into a bouquet to admire. Continually maintaining your garden will ensure a constant rotation of bouquets over time.

Section 1

LET Yourself Bloom

"You deserve to bloom, not break."[2]
—Rithvik Singh

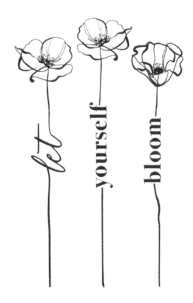

---

[2] Rithvik Singh Rathore, on his Instagram page (@wordsofrithvik), September 21, 2021.

ONE
DIVINE GENIUS:
Soil

(Nutrients Are Strengths)

"Too often we compare our weaknesses with other people's strengths only to find ourselves coming up short."[3]

–Ruth Schwenk

---

[3] Ruth Schwenk, *From Grouchy to Great: Finding Joy in the Journey of Motherhood*, (North Charleston: CreateSpace Independent Publishing Platform, 2017).

The first applied step in a garden is testing the soil. Testing your soil is like checking a recipe before cooking—it helps you make sure you have all the right "ingredients" for your plants to thrive. A soil test can offer insights into fertility, health, and suitability for growth. I will be walking you through how to test your soil's nutrients: your strengths.

In the past, I didn't understand how my strengths applied to real-life situations beyond that of a job. The talents and competencies I had developed in my personal life seemed unrelated to the challenges and responsibilities of being a wife, mother, and member of society. There were moments of happiness throughout my life, but even *existing* is an intense job, so those moments were easy to miss. When I am enjoying life, it is because I am utilizing my strengths and innate talents. This leads to enriched soil—the more nutrients that are cycled into soil, the more fertile the ground will become.

One day, my therapist had me think about a time when I felt like I was on top of the world—a time when I felt true joy, felt most like myself, and things were going my way. What came to mind was my first year of college. I felt like I had a blank slate, that I could portray myself in any way I chose. I had a little bit of responsibility but a lot of newfound freedom. I made a lot of new friends. It was a very exciting time in my life.

Normally, we think about identity formation happening only in adolescence. However, every life change can necessitate a reevaluation of who we are. No wonder I felt on top of the world during my first year of college! This was a peak time of discovering who I was. I had a similar experience nearly ten years and three kids later: motherhood was when I began another identity journey. Many people have called these experiences identity "crises." We can replace the word "crisis" with "journey." What brought you to identity exploration? There are many paths to a singular destination.

The question in my mind during my motherhood identity exploration was, *what is a "good mom" anyway?* I used to nebulously strive to be a "good mom," wandering around and getting nowhere. As information has become more accessible, societal programming has increased. We absorb what other people are doing and often use it against ourselves. We research and question, and we compare what we're doing against what others are doing, which then creates guilt.

MomSquad Secrets

Change your perspective. Motherhood is not a job, it's a calling. —Sarah Z.

Resist the urge to compare your child to others, a developmental app, or even to siblings. —Heather

Parent the child you have, not the child you wish you had. — Kira

Have fun with your kids! Be young again. —Casey

When asked what my goal is as a parent, I always reply, "for my children to no longer need me around but still very much want me around." —Kylie

Societal pressure can cause you to feel like you have to be a contortionist, conforming into the shape of the stereotype. However,

"It's a rare baseball player who is equally good at every position. Why should a natural third baseman labor to develop his skills as a right fielder?"[4]

When you play to your strengths, you thrive within your sphere of influence. The way you decide to *be* is your business alone; no one will do it the exact same way you do. If you follow your intuition instead of societal programming, you will be the member of society you are meant to contribute as, the partner someone looks up to, and the mother your children need. No two snowflakes are alike, so why should two people be alike? The paths you choose in life create a journey tailored for your growth and for the growth of those around you. There are many environments that are ideal conditions for growth.

When I would hear someone share what they do personally or in their home, my immediate habit was to judge it against what I was doing. I would think, "Oh no, I 'should' be doing it that way. What if that's the best way to do it? What if I'm doing it wrong?" As I've slowed it down, I am able to check in personally, thus interrupting the pattern of comparison. I note what feels right for me and my situation. I remember to follow the advice of Emily P. Freeman to "stop collecting gurus."[5]

---

[4] Laura Morgan Roberts et al, "How To Play to Your Strengths," *Harvard Business Review*, January 2005, https://hbr.org/2005/01/how-to-play-to-your-strengths.

[5] Emily P. Freeman, "Stop Collecting Gurus," *The Next Right Thing* podcast, episode 32, April 10, 2018, https://emilypfreeman.com/podcast/32/.

For example, different approaches to managing screen time and fostering learning in children can lead to feelings of guilt and doubt in parenting decisions, even when the chosen method is thoughtfully balanced and tailored to the child's needs. One mother may limit screen time to educational games and TV shows and balance this with reading books and outdoor activities. Another mother may emphasize minimal screen time and place a heavy focus on reading. The former, despite seeing the positive impact and enjoyment her child derives from his screen time, feels guilty and worries she should be encouraging more reading. Comparisons can undermine a parent's confidence in their well-considered choices.

Living externally in alignment with your internal strengths—living as your authentic self—will not only boost your confidence and effectiveness but will also open the door to discovering your **Divine Genius—the unique talents and insights that set you apart and drive your purpose.** When you learn to let go of all that doesn't serve you (often societal pressure), you are able to channel your energy into a singular internal focus.

There is a portion of Divine Genius within you. Some refer to it as their "calling" or "life's purpose." What it really comes down to is **an ability that comes naturally, the essence of your soul.** Can you choose a *title* that reflects that? Whether your fulfillment comes from within the home or without, you can reframe your responsibilities in a way that ignites your energy instead of extinguishing it.

Divine Genius is your ground; healthy soil is crucial in supporting life. When you have a good environment from which to grow, you are more resilient to the external impacts that may present themselves. When you have a different title as your starting point, you can be reminded of the other identifiers and purposes you have. It's discouraging to feel depleted before you even begin your day.

I prefer the title of "office manager" as my role in the home. It takes the pressure off my "mom" title so that I can show up for the nurturing and connective moments when they arise. Motherhood feels so vast and unknown. Office manager seems more concrete and doable in my mind. I'm able to view it as a defined role with actionable tasks.

For you, "office manager" may sound terrible. That's because it's not the right fit for you. Maybe you enjoy more of an activity coordinator role. Or you prefer mentoring. The point is to recognize what fills you up, and then you can do that within your home; it can be part of your enriched soil. You may notice some big boulders, or obstacles, that need to be dealt with before your soil is ready for planting. In Chapter Nine we will talk about removing these obstacles.

If you're having a hard time identifying your Divine Genius (natural strengths and abilities), consider using the Reflected Best Self (RBS) Exercise (found in the article "How to Play to Your Strengths" on the *Harvard Business Review* website: https://hbr.org/2005/01/how-to-play-to-your-strengths).

The Reflected Best Self Exercise is a powerful way to see your strengths in a different light. During the RBS exercise, you'll reach outward and compile and condense feedback from people who have seen you at your best in varying stages of your life, both personal and professional.

Ask those who are closest to you to name the strengths they see in you. Review the information and use it as an indication of a title that could be a better fit for you in your current role at work, in a relationship, as a mother, or in a volunteer position. If it's a fit, spend some time praying, meditating, or journaling as a way to help to identify your strengths.

Having a fertile ground is the first step to ensuring a healthy, thriving garden. Your title can change over time, depending on your growing season. You may recognize the need to adjust your role according to a change in responsibilities.

If you want to choose a new role, start by naming a few of your strengths. Then, convert these into a title. This is how you name your Divine Genius. Don't get too caught up in choosing "the right" one. Test a couple and see how they feel as your Divine Genius, or Divine Ground.

Testing Your Soil: Naming Your Strengths (Nutrients)	
Examples of Strengths	Corresponding Title
Planning, organizing, scheduling	Architect of the Future
Having empathy, compassion, patience	Love Instiller
Teaching, mentoring, asking open-ended questions	Soul Coach
Encouraging independence, fostering problem-solving, building confidence	Self-Reliance Cultivator

Listening actively, providing emotional support, validating feelings	Heart Healer
Setting boundaries, establishing routines, remaining consistent in discipline	Stability Designer
Engaging in creative play, imaginative activities, and artistic expression	Creativity Cultivator
Incorporating healthy eating, physical activity, and wellness promotion	Wellness Warrior
Telling stories, sharing traditions, connecting with ancestors	Heritage Keeper
Leading nature exploration, environmental awareness, and outdoor activities	Nature Guide
Encouraging social interaction, teaching cooperation, building friendships	Social Connector
Encouraging curiosity, providing learning opportunities, stimulating intellectual growth	Learning Facilitator
Embodying humor, joy, playfulness, and an ability to create fun memories	Joy Bringer
Encouraging self-expression, supporting unique interests, fostering individuality	Individuality Advocate
Teaching financial literacy, encouraging responsibility, instilling work ethic	Future Financier

My New Title: _____

I am inviting you to think about how important it is to know and nurture your core values. Imagine your values as seeds you're planting in your own garden. When you take the time to plant these seeds carefully, they take root and grow strong. By recognizing your strengths, you're creating a solid foundation for your personal growth and happiness.

Each of your strengths is a part of what makes you unique. Embrace these natural abilities and let them guide you. Whether you find joy inside the home or out in the world, framing your responsibilities in a way that excites you will help you thrive.

Take a moment to think about how you can bring your strengths and values into every part of your life. When you do this, you not only feel better yourself but you also positively affect those around you. Remember, your garden is yours to care for, and the seeds you plant with love and intention will grow into something beautiful.

As you go forward, keep checking in with yourself and making changes as needed. Stay committed to your growth, and let your core values lead the way. Your life's garden is a testament to your amazing potential, and with each season you have the chance to bloom even more.

Bloom Tip:

We're already so hard on ourselves. If we see motherhood (or any other role) as too enormous to aspire to, we'll want to quit when we've barely started. Without a concrete idea of where we're going, we won't know when we've arrived. Define what motherhood looks like for YOU so you know when you've reached your ideal.

Definition of a "good" mother:

_____

_____

_____

_____

TWO
PLANTING THE SEEDS:
Germination

(Seeds Are Core Values)

"Values are like fingerprints. Nobody's are the same, but you leave 'em all over everything you do."

—**Elvis Presley**
(widely attributed, source unknown)

Identifying what means most to you will guide your life and liberate you from all you carry, and I am here to help you identify what means most to you. Imagine your core values as seeds in your garden. When we carry too many seeds in our hands, we risk dropping them, misplacing them, or forgetting about them altogether. However, when we carefully plant these seeds in a dedicated garden plot labeled "core values," those seeds take root and flourish. When each value is neatly organized with a sign in its own designated row, it becomes readily accessible whenever we need to draw upon it.

Core values are the way you view life. They govern your opinions, beliefs, and frustrations—whether you can name the core values or not. Many of your core values have been there since childhood. You may not always "choose" your core values; you may just need to uncover your values from within your soil and name them. If you concern yourself with everything, you may find that you truly prioritize nothing. I'll give you a few core value examples and then you can pick and choose what resonates with you and narrow that list down to name just three to five core value seeds to help you grow.

My core value seeds are:

1. Connection
2. Contribution
3. Reliability
4. Refinement

When I found these core values, my life stopped being hectic and started to be guided. Knowing my core values started the germination process on my path to blooming. **Germination is the development of a plant from a seed after a period of dormancy.** Some women may feel their identity is dormant within motherhood. Once the ground is prepared, and the seeds are viable, your identity can be reframed through the process of naming your core values.

To name my core values, I went through a list of core values from Brené Brown's book, *Dare to Lead* and placed a star by any that stuck out to me. I also crossed out any that were an obvious no. I grouped words that were similar to identify overarching themes. From there, I circled words that still stuck out and narrowed my core values down to four. In narrowing down and naming your core values, you could sort the values with a value deck that you purchase or print out or write the values on pieces of paper.

My first core value is **connection**. I love gatherings of all kinds and being around people; I consider myself an extrovert but especially love when I can connect personally with various individuals. Other similar values that resonated were belonging, collaboration, community, cooperation, friendship, openness, and teamwork. To me, connection looks like moving past small talk, sharing both the good and the hard, feeling seen, and the moments I say, "Me too."

My next core value is **contribution**. Because I wasn't feeling fulfilled inside the home as a stay-at-home mother, the values of achievement, ambition, contribution, freedom, fun, generosity, independence, initiative, personal fulfillment, and service stuck out to me. I wanted a word that signified making a difference beyond what I was accomplishing at home. To me, contribution looks like adding to a cause bigger than myself, influencing the lives of others, making quantifiable change, and giving generously.

Reliability is my third core value. Growing up, the importance of being on time was modeled over and over. I internalized the practice of showing up early and brought it into my adult life. It was also instilled that, in my family, we could be counted on; we kept our promises and commitments. Due to my upbringing and what I had subsequently learned was important, I selected the values of commitment, efficiency, excellence, loyalty, order, responsibility, and self-discipline. To me, reliability means following through on what I said I would do, making myself available, managing my mind, and being respectful and true to who I am.

My fourth core value is **refinement**. When I was twelve, I began collecting inspirational quotes. Mentors gave me handouts filled with wisdom and I wanted a place to record all of the profound words I was hearing. I began writing them down in the back of a notebook. I then moved to typing them on the computer, altering the fonts and colors, and printing them out when I had a full page. I would glue them into a journal, and my collection grew. I believe these quotes are the reason I'm drawn to self-improvement. The related values were authenticity, growth, leadership, perseverance, resourcefulness, self-expression, self-realization, and uniqueness. To me, refinement looks like continuous learning, growing into the next version of myself, being concise, and naming the essentials.

The first two values were the easiest for me to determine, whereas the other two took a bit longer to put into words. I also stopped at four instead of looking for a fifth because I liked how two began with the letter *c* and two began with the letter *r*. I am open to seeing if these change over time, but for now they feel like the best fit.

Core values can be both descriptive and aspirational but will mostly convey who you are currently. If over half of your core values are attributes you hope to obtain, you risk feeling "shoulds" and guilt.

As soon as you name your core values, you'll begin observing other people making choices as if those choices are associated with a core value. It's important to note that we are not talking about values as standards of behavior, rather, one's judgment of what's important in life. Core values are morally neutral; certain values are not better than others. This knowledge helps you avoid judging others so you can be who you are and allow others to do the same.

When someone was late for an appointment, I would think to myself, "Even though they don't have the value of reliability at this moment, they are living life according to their core values, and that's okay." It's easy to judge people based on your core values because that's how you see the world. We only have a glimpse of what's really going on in their life and don't often see the big picture. Maybe right beforehand they were valuing patience with their children over rushing to be on time.

MomSquad Secret

Everything takes longer to do. Add a ten-minute buffer per child to get out the door. —Jen

Knowing your core values and being able to recall them instantly will help guide your decisions and help you to focus on what truly matters to you. We will be referring back to our list of core values throughout the book, so once you've named yours, keep the list nearby.

Core Values List: Brené Brown, *Dare to Lead*[6]

Accountability
Achievement
Adaptability
Adventure
Altruism
Ambition
Authenticity
Balance
Beauty
Being the best
Belonging
Career
Caring
Collaboration
Commitment
Community
Compassion
Competence
Confidence
Connection
Contentment
Contribution
Cooperation

---

6 Brené Brown, *Dare to Lead: Brave Work. Tough Conversations. Whole Hearts* (New York: Random House, 2018).

Courage
Creativity
Curiosity
Dignity
Diversity
Environment
Efficiency
Equality
Ethics
Excellence
Fairness
Faith
Family
Financial stability
Forgiveness
Freedom
Friendship
Fun
Future generations
Generosity
Giving back
Grace
Gratitude
Growth
Harmony
Health
Home
Honesty
Hope
Humility
Humor
Inclusion

Independence
Initiative
Integrity
Intuition
Job security
Joy
Justice
Kindness
Knowledge
Leadership
Learning
Legacy
Leisure
Love
Loyalty
Making a difference
Nature
Openness
Optimism
Order
Parenting
Patience
Patriotism
Peace
Perseverance
Personal fulfillment
Power
Pride
Recognition
Reliability
Resourcefulness
Respect

Responsibility
Risk -taking
Safety
Security
Self-discipline
Self-expression
Self-respect
Serenity
Service
Simplicity
Spirituality
Sportsmanship
Stewardship
Success
Teamwork
Thrift
Time
Tradition
Travel
Trust
Truth
Understanding
Uniqueness
Usefulness
Vision
Vulnerability
Wealth
Well-being
Wholeheartedness
Wisdom

Write your own:

_____

_____

_____

My 3–5 Core Value Seeds

(We will be referring back to this list throughout the book)

1._____

2._____

3._____

4._____

5._____

As you embark on the journey of identifying and nurturing your core values, remember that these values are the seeds of your life's garden. Plant them with intentionality, care, and attention. Just as a gardener tends to each plant, ensuring it has the right conditions to grow, you must cultivate your values and let them guide your actions and decisions.

By focusing on your core values, you create a solid foundation for your identity and a clear path for your personal growth. These values will help you navigate life's challenges, celebrate its joys, and maintain a sense of purpose and direction. As you nurture these seeds, you'll find that your life becomes more balanced, fulfilling, and aligned with who you truly are.

Bloom Tip:

Plant your core values with care and nurture them daily. They will help you grow and thrive in all parts of your life.

Remember, your garden is yours to cultivate. Embrace your core values, let them take root, and watch as they grow into beautiful, thriving identity flowers that reflect your true self. With each value you nurture, you bloom into the best version of yourself, ready to face the world with confidence, clarity, and joy.

THREE

THE SECRET TO
STEADY GROWTH:

Watering

(Soul-care)

"A waterfall starts with just one drop of water."[7]

Picture a seed, deep below the surface; it feels hopeless, alone in the
dark . . . wondering what could possibly be the purpose of this

---

[7] *The Power of One*, Directed by John G. Avildsen, distributed by Warner
Bros. Pictures, released March 27, 1992 (USA).

seemingly dreary life. What the seed doesn't know is that it's in the exact conditions needed for growth. The very soil that feels suffocating is what will allow the seed to crack open and bloom.

Planting a seed is only the first step. Let's celebrate that you're taking that step! Or maybe you planted some seeds in the past, and now you're ready to start watering them. There has always been potential within that seed, but maybe it was dormant for a time. Now that the germination process has begun, the seed is eager to continue to develop. Water is essential in the overall growth of the flower.

MomSquad Secret

When your children are born, you enter the physical stage of motherhood: changing diapers, feeding them, interpreting needs, carrying. Children require a lot. You may lose yourself—for a time. However, there are small ways you can feel like yourself within motherhood.

One specific day sticks out in my mind. It was the day after Halloween, right before dinner—the "witching" hour. It was overcast and rainy, but my middle son asked to ride his bike. I told him it was too wet to go out, and he began to cry as a result of being told "no." My oldest son asked for yet another piece of Halloween candy, and I told him we needed to eat dinner before consuming any more sweets. He stomped off to the corner and began to cry as well. My baby joined in, partly because of all the crying, and also because it was time for him to eat too. I had to go to the bathroom. Dinner still wasn't ready. I walked away from the chaos, locked the bathroom door, and took a few breaths to help me feel like myself again. While in the bathroom, I also sent out an S.O.S text to a friend group asking for what helped them get through the dinner hour. At that moment, I had zero headspace for thinking of solutions because I was in crisis mode. My friends came to the rescue with helpful suggestions and survival skills. I wrote their ideas on a sticky note and put it on my fridge for the future when it was likely to happen again.

Suggestions I received:

— Offer a bucket of water and cups for your children to play in.

— Prep dinner earlier in the day to make the dinner hour smoother.

— Set expectations beforehand (for both you and your children).

— Have an "out-of-the-norm" activity to try (like noodle-threading on string).

— Play some fun music.

— Set aside a treat just for you while you make dinner.

As your children grow older, you enter the emotional stage of motherhood: talking through matters of self-esteem, teaching morals, navigating choices, and holding conversations about how life works. It can become even more mentally taxing. Sometimes, we don't have the bandwidth to address our own needs as we're meeting theirs. Fortunately, if we prepare a list of soul-care activities ahead of time, it will be readily available when we're feeling depleted.

Soul-care is one of the best ways to maintain our identity. A lot of the time, we think of the commercialized or indulgent forms of self-care, and while there is a time and a place for those, soul-care encompasses the broader categories of body, mind, and spirit. Soul-care doesn't have to take a lot of time; there are ways to experience it in small doses that take only a minute. You would never water a plant once during its lifetime and then call it good; it needs water often. Similarly, a little bit of soul-care everyday, over time, will fill us up so we can then give what's overflowing to our children. As you're nurturing your children, nurture you as well. Drink as you're watering.

> True [soul-care] is not salt baths and chocolate cake. It's making the choice to **build a life** *you don't need to regularly escape from.*
>
> If you find yourself having to regularly indulge in consumer self-care, it might be because you are disconnected from actual self-care, which has very little to do with "treating yourself" and a whole lot to do with parenting yourself and making choices for your long-term wellness.
>
> It is no longer using your hectic and unreasonable life as justification for self-sabotage . . . It is learning how to stop trying to "fix yourself" and start trying to take care of yourself . . . and maybe finding that taking

care lovingly attends to a lot of the problems you were trying to fix in the first place.

It means being the hero of your life, not the victim. It means rewiring what you have until your everyday life isn't something that you need therapy to recover from. It is no longer choosing a life that looks good over a life that feels good. It is giving the hell up on some goals so you can care about others. It is being honest even if that means you aren't universally liked. It is meeting your own needs so you aren't anxious and dependent on other people.

It is becoming the person you know you want and are meant to be. Someone who knows that salt baths and chocolate cake are ways to enjoy life—not escape from it.[8]

I know how hard it is to come up with ideas because right now you're exhausted, you're depleted, and the last thing you want to do is even *think* about what could be soul-care for you. I've prepared some suggestions below. Included in the list are one-minute, five-minute, half-hour, and hour-long activities that are soul-care (mind, body, and spirit). These are essentials, not weeds. If your seeds do not get water, they will not grow. Over time, as you experiment with this list, add to it or create your own table.

---

[8] Brianna Weist, "This Is What Self-Care Really Means, Because It's Not all Salt Baths and Chocolate Cake," *Thought Catalog*, April 17, 2024, https://thoughtcatalog.com/brianna-wiest/2024/04/this-is-what-self-care-really-means-because-its-not-all-salt-baths-and-chocolate-cake-2/.

One Minute	Five Minutes	30 Minutes	One Hour
Dance to a favorite song.	Watch the sunrise.	Go for a walk.	Take a nap.
5-5-5 Breathing: In for five seconds, hold for five seconds, out for five seconds Repeat as desired. Can also do 7-7-7	1. Notice your breath. 2. Picture your thoughts and to-dos like a raging river. 3. Picture the river getting calmer and then smaller. 4. Continue with your day, one step at a time.	Follow a 30-minute guided meditation from the internet.	Spend time in nature or go to a shopping mall to walk.
		Do yoga, ride a bike, do an internet dance video, swim.	Plan an event or an upcoming vacation.
		Converse with a friend or write in a journal.	Meditate, reflect, set goals, look at pictures.
Tell yourself an affirmation.	Brain dump on a notepad.	Read, do a puzzle, draw.	Take a social media fast.
Name three things you are grateful for.	Enjoy a fun homemade drink.	Listen to a podcast.	Try something new (class, activity).
Give a compliment.	Declutter a small space.	Try a new recipe.	Do a craft.
Do 10 jumping jacks.	Pick or buy flowers.	Watch a TED talk.	Play!
Have a little treat.	Write a note.	Work standing up.	Participate in therapy.

You can scan the QR code below to download a printable version of this table

Bloom Tip:

Soul-care is not a luxury, it's a necessity. —Mary B.

Watering Your Soul

If your cup is full, you'll bring a different energy to life than if it's empty. Many mothers don't enjoy feeling "bothered" by their children. When you're feeling "bothered," it is often a signal that you have some unmet needs. Ask the following questions whenever you're feeling bothered:

— *How do I feel?*

— *What do I want?*

These two questions are another great window into your unique desires. Tapping into them will allow you to alter the energy you're experiencing and be present in the current moment. You can't always avoid feeling bothered by others, but you can definitely influence how often it affects your energy.

We're not going to be perfect at implementing this preventative measure. One particular day, my fuse was quite a bit shorter than usual. My cup was not full—I had not been as intentional with self-care. One of my children asked me a question and my anger bubbled right up to the surface. I said a silent prayer to help me through the moment, and I felt my anger evaporate in seconds as if it had turned into steam. I was able to calmly respond to my child, but that situation required a power beyond my own. My least favorite way to parent is from anger or stress. The more aware I am of my own energy levels, the more leverage I have over whether I'm reacting or responding.

It's also tempting to bring an old version (old energy) of your SELF to a new season in life. If you're used to working out at a gym for several hours at a time and now you have a newborn, you will likely have to adjust your expectations and way of working out. You can't fit a triangle into a square hole. Finding small ways to exercise throughout the day will, over time, help you continue to feel like your SELF. The more in tune you are with yourself, the easier it will be to use your SELF as a filter for what you do and incorporate. You'll be able to say, confidently, "That feels right." Right to you, devoid of comparison.

Another insight into energy is Human Design—a roadmap for how you live life.[9] Understanding your body's energy reserves and flow, especially in relation to those with whom you live and interact, can help you determine if and when you're feeling depleted.

MomSquad Secret

Take care of yourself first during moments of transition. When you arrive back home or before you leave the house, take care of your needs so you're better able to address other needs that arise. —Ali L.

Within the shell of a seed lies everything it needs to grow. By watering it, you provide the catalyst for the seed's transformation. Now it can crack open and bloom.

Bloom Tip:

Just as a seed needs water to grow, regularly nurture your own needs and passions to bloom fully. Consistent soul-care replenishes your energy, allowing you to thrive and bring your best self to every role you play. Schedule at least one soul-care item per day.

---

[9] For more information, see "Human Design" on Wikipedia, https://en.wikipedia.org/wiki/Human_Design.

FOUR
BLOSSOMS:
Goals

(Always Keep
Your Garden in Bloom)

"A goal without a plan is just a wish."[10]

—**Antoine de Saint-Exupéry**

---

[10] Antoine de Saint-Exupéry, *Le Petit Prince*, (Paris, France: Gallimard, 1943).

After I graduated from college, I taught in a public school for a few years while my husband was in law school. As soon as he was done with school, I left the profession. During this time of transition, I felt aimless. I definitely enjoyed the respite from teaching and was enjoying time with my little ones, but life felt different than it had up to that point. I had always kept a vision or plan in front of me as I progressed toward whichever finish line was in my near future. At this time, my nearest goal was starting an in-home preschool, but we didn't yet own a home and didn't know when we would, so my goal didn't have a plan attached to it.

A life coach who lived in my neighborhood—Sherry Fernandez, author of *Life Mastery*—began teaching free webinars. One of the first lessons was creating a personal mission statement. The word I had chosen as my New Year's resolution was "curate." My initial purpose statement followed this template:

To use my_____(resourcefulness)_____
strengths, talents, skills, virtues (i.e. what I have to offer the world)
by _____(gathering others)_____
verbs, short, concise (i.e. how I'll do it) so that ____(they____are
empowered to curate their lives)____ultimate goal, effect (i.e. what impact I hope to make)

Put together, this would read:

To use my resourcefulness by gathering others so that they are empowered to curate their lives.

You can also distill it down to just one word (verb) so it's easier to recall: gather or curate in this instance.

In determining my personal mission statement and purpose word for my current stage, I first decide on my purpose word and then form my mission statement. Today that looks like this:

Purpose Word: Liberator

Personal Mission Statement: To utilize my personal refinement experiences by liberating women so that they can achieve their fullest potential, find balance, and grow in their self-awareness.

There was another time in my life when I had so many goals I was working on simultaneously that I felt like I was on an intense roller coaster with no end in sight and no way to get off. Balance is key in the pursuit of goals (more on this in the next chapter).

Bloom Tip:

Don't sit on your to-do list for ages. The reason things remain on our to-do list is that they're too big of tasks. Break them down into small, digestible actions.

To enhance your bouquet and add variety, regularly introduce to your garden new identity flowers: your goals. When it's time to harvest your bouquets, you will want to have a cycle of flowers growing, whether they are annuals or perennials. Setting new goals, or maintaining the same goals, will keep your garden continuously in bloom so that there are always flowers to harvest. How do we set a goal and incorporate it into our daily life? Here is where we begin planting. Just like we planted our core values, we can plant each goal anew for it to become an identity flower. The following process is how you can ensure that the seeds you sow grow to maturity.

> *"If you want to be happy, set a goal that commands your thoughts, liberates your energy, and inspires your hopes."*
>
> **–Andrew Carnegie**
> **(widely attributed, source unknown)**

"Commands Your Thoughts" Process

You could talk about your chosen goal for hours. You are constantly receiving new thoughts and ideas to fuel it. When you have quiet moments, it's all you think about. You're aware of relevant information because what you focus on expands. By integrating your goal into your daily life, it becomes a part of who you are, much like an identity flower in your garden. This focus helps your goal flourish and keeps your life in a perpetual state of growth and renewal.

For me, an area where this happens is event planning. My highest core value is connection, so I seek any and every fitting opportunity to *gather*. While I love casual get-togethers and spontaneous outings, it brings me great joy to plan an event from conception to actualization. Like travelers who plan their next vacation on the way home from a trip, I don't let very much time, if any, go by between events, and I am often planning several simultaneously. I'm known to plan my boys' birthday parties a year in advance! As soon as I have an idea for an event, it's deliciously invigorating to think through every last detail.

My ultimate goal is to own an event center. Renting it out for others to use would be a happy by-product, but I would want to possess it so I could selfishly use it as often as I wanted for my own purposes. I envision holding workshops, storytelling nights, soul-care events, celebrations, recitals, and anything else that may come to mind.

Capture, Categorize, Create

Setting goals can sometimes feel overwhelming, which is why the process of capture, categorize, create will support your goals. Historically, I've used the notes app on my phone to record the influx of information pouring into my brain (capture). This works very well in the short term. After a while, I print out the notes and file them (categorize) to reduce the digital clutter on my phone. I then use the information to make a product, design a course, craft a speech, or keep for future use (create). When you learn how to capture, categorize, and create with your goals, you will feel liberated and energized! No more goals left behind and the frustration of too many ideas being lost will end. You will begin to see your goal transpire into reality!

Your turn to watch your goals sprout.

Capture

What is one thing that has been sprouting in your thoughts this past month?

_____

_____

_____

_____

_____

Water the seeds. Write down what thoughts begin to grow in your mind. How can you structure your soul-care so you can continually cultivate these ideas?

_____

_____

_____

_____

_____

Categorize

What are the branches of these thought patterns? In other words, how can you group them?

_____

_____

_____

_____

_____

_____

Create

How can you create something to bloom as a result?

_____

_____

_____

_____

_____

_____

"Liberates Your Energy" Process

Your goal is life-giving rather than life-draining. You can't wait to get started or continue working on it. You fantasize about spending more of your time in this area and want to share updates about it in a journal or with another person.

An example of something that is life-giving for me is book club, where I spend quality time once a month in laughter and meaningful conversations that nourish my soul. My second core value is contribution, so I assist in planning the monthly agenda as well as annual retreats, and I immensely enjoy those meetings and processes. When I participate in an activity that is life-draining—like one of my volunteer positions—I often dread the meetings and interactions required of me. Constantly engaging in toxic relationships and dominating environments sap my energy and leave me feeling depleted.

Your turn to nourish the seeds of your goal.

Make a list of activities that are life-giving vs. life-draining

Life-giving *Ex: Book club, close friends*	Life-draining *Ex: Volunteer meetings, one person dominates*

Reflect: Do you have a goal that is life-giving or life-draining?

_____

_____

_____

_____

_____

_____

Bloom Tip:

If it's life-giving, think of one way you can incorporate it more into your life. If it's life-draining, think of ways you can reduce how it impacts your life.

I can incorporate my life-giving goal more into my life by: _____

_____

_____

_____

I can reduce the ways life-draining goals impact my life by: _____

_____

_____

_____

"Inspires Your Hopes" Process

The goal you're working toward makes the problems in your life seem smaller. It gives you a reason to wake up feeling excited in the morning. You start to manifest it in your life because of the positivity you're fostering toward it.

I know that sometimes the need to do it perfectly stops people from taking action. There will be a "messy middle." Don't be afraid to make mistakes because there's actually no such thing as "doing it wrong." Take the leaps forward! You won't regret it.

I had a friend commend me for not being afraid of the messy middle. When we just take the first step, any step, we gain momentum and become the magnet for success. When I'm engaged in a project or goal, I'm invigorated.

My first podcast was a complete DIY adventure. I googled the steps to get started, did a bit of research on the best platforms and audio equipment, then I wrote and recorded my first few episodes. I didn't spend more time than was necessary to begin. I knew that I'd get better as I went along so the faster I started, the faster I would get my not-so-ideal episodes out of the way.

Bloom Tip:

There's a point when you research too much. Educate yourself to get an answer, along with your intuition, and then don't overthink it. —Eva

A few years later, my friend Sarah and I collaborated on *The Best Birth* podcast miniseries. It was exciting to reach out to sponsors, guests, partners, and audience members because it was an endeavor bigger than ourselves. It was easier this go-around because I'd done the work beforehand to get started. If you wait five years to get started, you lose five years of progress and growth.

Your turn to help your seeds grow.

Write down 5–10 things you're grateful for.

_____

_____

_____

_____

_____

_____

_____

_____

_____

_____

"Plant a seed of [gratitude], reap a bouquet of happiness." [11]

---

[11] Lois L. Kaufman quoted in BJ Gallagher, *Friends Are Everything: The Power of Female Friendship*, (Newbury Port: Conari Press, 2022), 5. Original quote is, "Plant a seed of friendship, reap a bouquet of happiness."

Have you ever said to yourself, everything's been done before, so why bother? Everything has been thought of, written, invented, accomplished—so why try, right? **Wrong! It hasn't been done by YOU.** You have a unique set of strengths, experiences, core values, talents, and personality traits that can't be replicated. When you bring your insights, vision, and expertise to a situation, you make a mark and leave behind your personal brand. Goals also refine and stretch us into the person we're meant to be.

The only way to actually accomplish something is to take genuine action—not the illusion of action. This means going beyond merely thinking, planning, or busy work. While those things are often important, they're not the meat of actually completing the small tasks that lead us to our eventual goal. True progress comes from actively working toward your goals and taking tangible steps forward.

Once your goal has grown, it is now one of your identity flowers. Remember to live in your own season. People may tell you it's "not the right time" but you know your season best. Maybe it is exactly the right time! When it is a harder season, you need goals and soul-care the most. Remember, just like in nature, **nothing blooms all year round.**

You can start out with one to two goals to make this become a part of your life. Then, I am inviting you to think bigger! Dream on a larger scale: always have fifty to one hundred things on your bucket list at any given time. Include items that you want to have, things you want to do, the person you want to be.

Write these goals and dreams down as if they're already true.

Examples:

> I have gotten Lasik eye surgery.
>
> I rode in a hot air balloon.
>
> I am a public speaker.
>
> What are some of the things you have on your bucket list?

Name five right now.

1._____

2._____

3._____

4._____

5._____

In an entrepreneurial roundtable discussion, John St. Pierre, author of *The $100M Journey*, shared that his initial step with clients is to develop a thirty-year plan. He emphasized that there is ample time for growth and no need to constantly rush. My rearview mirror ornament depicts a sloth along with the words, "Don't hurry, be happy."

By continually setting and nurturing your goals, you ensure that your garden of identity flowers is always in bloom. Your dreams and aspirations are unique to you, and the world needs your individual contribution. Remember, the only way to truly accomplish something is to take genuine action. Thinking, planning, and busy work are necessary, but real progress comes from taking concrete steps forward.

Bloom Tip :

As you cultivate your garden over time, embrace the beauty of each season and keep your dreams alive. Your identity flowers will flourish, bringing color and vitality to your life. Stay focused, stay inspired, and let your garden grow at its *own* pace.

Your journey is yours to shape. Plant your seeds, water them with care, and watch as your dreams blossom into reality.

Section 2

Let YOURSELF Bloom

"Be yourself. You are the most qualified."
—**Unknown**

FIVE
ROOM TO BLOOM:
Greenhouses

(Give Yourself Space)

"He who trims himself to suit everyone will soon
whittle himself away."

—Raymond Hull
(widely attributed, original source unknown)

Do you remember a time in your life when you felt taken care of? I
want you to focus on how it felt to be cared for and nurtured. This is
what we get to do for our goals.

In this chapter, we are going to focus on how to nurture and care for your goals. Greenhouses are a unique place to tend to plants in conditions specifically engineered for optimal growth. They are ideal environments formulated to help plants be their best. Inside, there are fewer bugs, no inconveniences, and an overall sense of order. I am going to help you nurture your identities in a greenhouse, so to speak. Visualize removing distractions, being present, and basking in the peacefully fragrant environment. That is what I am going to help you do for your goals!

I once overheard a conversation between a young adult and her mother-in-law. The younger woman was lamenting that she felt like her life was not going to *start* until she became a mother. The mother-in-law said in return that the young woman's life was going to *end* when she became a mother. Have you ever felt like you were waiting for your life to start?

Oftentimes, we wait for external circumstances to elicit the feelings we want to experience. "I'll be happy when X happens." "When I finish X, then I'll feel fulfilled." This young adult was viewing her life by what she lacked and by doing so was reserving her happiness for a future date. The mother-in-law was likely speaking from experience—perhaps she had felt like her life ended when she became a mother. And maybe it had, compared to the way she was living prior to motherhood. Both women had different perspectives based on their circumstances. Each had a perception of how the other would experience or had experienced life.

What are you waiting to feel? What happiness are you delaying because of your circumstances? Take a minute to think about these questions and write about them.

_____

_____

_____

_____

_____

_____

_____

Someone may want to lose weight because they believe it will make them feel more confident. Another may want to make a lot of money because they believe it will make them feel successful. Still another may want to be in a relationship because they believe it will make them feel loved. There is no magic switch once we've achieved a specific goal; we don't automatically feel differently once we've arrived. It's not the destination but the journey where we can make lasting changes.

Our identity is fluid. Who we are supersedes whatever we are currently doing. Can we just *be*, regardless of our stage in life? One of my favorite words in the English language is "become." There's so much possibility and potential in that one word. It was my favorite long before I had children. In the world, there is so much focus on having and doing but what about *being*?

I used to base my worth on my achievements, which was often what I had gotten *done* in a day. As I stacked each brick of accomplishment and task, I built a fortress that became my prison. "Look, I did so much! I cleaned a closet, went to work, made dinner, volunteered . . ." I used to be a victim to my lists, yet they were what I was most proud of. The need to prove my self-worth was perpetuated each time someone asked, "What did you *do* today?" I didn't feel like just "being" was enough.

With inventions to speed up productivity and conveniences brought about throughout history, we have gotten very efficient as a society. However, with that comes the filling up of the space of time we worked hard to create . . . with even more work! People are literally working themselves to death. We do it to make ourselves feel like we have worth because of our lists and daily accomplishments.

If you didn't have to prove your worth, who would you want to be? How would you spend your day? Who do you want to become? Who do you want to show up as?

Take a minute to journal through these questions on the lines below:

_____

_____

_____

_____

_____

You're allowed to answer these questions *while you're a mother.* **You're allowed to take up space.** *You're allowed to dream.* **Motherhood is just one of your identity flowers.**

So often we're wrapped up in the story that motherhood **is** our identity; we've enmeshed the two together so much that we can't separate them. This point of view changes the way you perceive yourself and how others perceive you. This is where you can become boxed in by your limitations and can sometimes become a victim to motherhood.

Similarly, if motherhood is the only thing we're deeply involved in, and the only way we're measuring our success, it can lead to perpetual striving and feelings of inadequacy in an idealized or narrow role. When you broaden your areas of fulfillment, you can lift some of the pressure off of one role onto many areas including personal achievements, career goals, hobbies, and other passions. It also allows your influence to extend beyond motherhood, *and foster a more balanced and enriched life.*

Identity is self-defined and unique only to you. *Only you* know what makes you feel the most like yourself. When you stay true to that within motherhood, you're holding both—being a mom AND being yourself.

If you grew up in an environment like I did, where the end goal was motherhood, that core value heavily influenced your identity. Just like a greenhouse provides a controlled environment for growth and maximizes the nutrients received, our environment has a direct correlation to what we become. Greenhouses offer protection, stability, ideal growing conditions, and energy efficiency. When plants grow with the help of a greenhouse, their growing season is extended and they are more likely to thrive. You can find a new environment that will nurture the identity that you want to grow.

MomSquad Secrets

My friend spent a lot of time in bed for three months the year her youngest started kindergarten. She wasn't pregnant and she wasn't sick. She made a choice to celebrate the milestone. She decided to take a rest, hit pause, and revel in the aloneness and the quiet. She allowed herself to savor the moment, soak in the solitude, and truly rest before jumping into her side-hustle of interior design. She created a *greenhouse of seclusion* to redefine her identity in a new season.

Another friend, who is in the stage of grandmothering, does volunteer work every Friday and Saturday, specifically so that she is unavailable to babysit her grandchildren. She has expressed that she wants to see them on her terms and doesn't want to be boxed into a babysitting job each week. She chose the *greenhouse of contribution* to bloom and be herself without being tied down to a role she didn't want to take on.

When I was eight months pregnant with my second child, I started my own podcast. A few months leading up to it, I set aside time every Sunday to prepare episode content, learn the logistics of producing quality audio, and purchase the necessary equipment to record. I weaved into this hobby my love of quotes, life experiences, and advice for weathering the storms in our lives. I created *a greenhouse of self-expression and self-development.* Making space for my interests allowed me to nurture my creativity, foster personal growth within a new experience, and maintain my emotional well-being.

You can choose the areas in which you want to see growth. It is imperative that you select the greenhouses that will be most conducive to your passion or Divine Genius. Carving out time and space to *be* will allow you to bloom in your environment.

Greg McKeown teaches in his book *Essentialism* that the word "priority" was never meant to be pluralized. We try to hold so many things at once, and it's impossible. When we divide ourselves in too many directions, we are diluting our influence.

Do you let obligations, commitments, and activities creep in? Calendars can fill up almost without us noticing, if we are unintentional. What does it look like to hold your time as sacred? Once you identify your current priority, align your calendar to reflect that. I felt a bit guilty when I read about the definition of "priority," but McKeown goes on to say that the Way of the Essentialist is to try many different things so you can determine what matters most to you.[12] I was in three book clubs at one point but have now pared it down to one: the one that matters most in my current stage.

Many times, we allow the busy-ness of life to consume and overwhelm us. We bounce from stage to stage like a ping-pong ball—somewhat haphazardly and often without intention. Usually, it's "survival mode," but if we are desiring to move from surviving into thriving, we can build in a few *greenhouses* like those I shared about in the MomSquad Secrets. Doing this will ensure we replenish the nutrients that may have been lost by overextending our schedules and having more than one priority at a time.

MomSquad Secret

Do the dishes to do the dishes. That is to say, be present in the current moment, whatever you're doing. Have a singular focus at one time. Snuggle your baby to snuggle your baby. —Sara

Take your core values and give them a greenhouse in which to grow. If one of your core values is learning, can you enroll in a community class, watch a YouTube video, or read a book about a new subject to create *a greenhouse of continuing education*? Your commitment and intention is where the magic happens.

Can you place yourself in *a greenhouse of community*? Select one of the strengths you named in Chapter One, and find an interest group, club,

---

[12] Greg McKeown, *Essentialism: The Disciplined Pursuit of Less*, (New York City: Crown Currency, 2014).

or online forum related to it. Maybe healing comes naturally to you. Find a group that works with varying methods of well-being.

Maybe you're feeling a lack of happiness in your life at this time. Build *a greenhouse of joy.* In her book *The Power of Fun,* Catherine Price states that "**true fun** is the confluence of playfulness, connection, and flow."[13] Can you identify an activity that includes playfulness (doing an activity just for the sake of doing it), connection (to self and others), and flow (losing track of time)? What is something that is *true fun* for you?

Other times, we need to add a flowerpot within our greenhouse. For time scarcity, you may need to give your schedule a flowerpot. I have a few friends who are bakers and cake decorators. Each of them has followed a similar pattern in actively choosing how many orders to take on in a given month. This allows them to say, "I'm booked. My calendar is full." But they're the ones who set that limit of what "full" looks like for them and the life they want to create. The things we're involved in needn't fill us to our very brim or overextend us. You choose your containers! It's time to stop overbooking yourself. You don't get an award for how many commitments you have! It's okay to rest and just *be*! We control the pace of our lives. This book will help you become the greatest version of you, but please rest! You can hold both: becoming the greatest version of yourself AND resting.

Rest is essential for your nurturing, and yet, it is relative. I told my therapist that I wanted more margin in my day, more space as opposed

---

[13] Catherine Price, *The Power of Fun: How to Feel Alive Again*, (New York: Dial Press, reissue edition 2024).

to jumping from activity to activity in my schedule. She challenged me to question my interpretation of rest and said that we all experience rest differently. What is life-giving for me likely won't be life-giving for another. What I do know, though, is that when you're living in the area of your Divine Genius, rest will feel rejuvenating. That's why we are encouraged to "find a job you enjoy doing, and you will never have to work a day in your life."[14] It won't feel like burdensome work when it truly lights your fire. This isn't to say there's not a place for physical or strenuous activity. But what is it that we're making hard that doesn't have to be?

MomSquad Secrets

Find ways to get out of the house each day, even if it's just a walk to the mailbox. —Carla

Paper plates can be a lifesaver! —Hayley

Adjust your expectations of what you get done in one day. Put "brush your teeth" on your to-do list so you can cross one thing off today. —Cindy

You kept humans alive today! —Jessica

What does rest look like for you? Our bodies need different kinds of rejuvenation at different times. Tune inward to see if you could benefit

---

[14] Harvey Mackay, quoted in "Faces 'N' Places: Mustachioed Michael a Suspicious Shopper," *The Stars and Stripes (European Stars and Stripes,* May 4, 1989, Quote page 12, Column 4, Darmstadt, Hesse, Germany.

from a moment alone or a moment with a close friend, a breath of fresh air or a quick shut-eye, a creative expression or a journal entry.

You may need to employ the use of the words "I'm not available" in situations that may make your life more crowded than you prefer. No need to give an explanation or justification. Another phrase that is helpful is "I can't." In your head, you could finish the sentence: I can't "engage in that activity without compromising my happiness and well-being," or I can't "take part in that activity without sacrificing my peace of mind and balance."

Below, identify a greenhouse or area of your life, goals, or core values that you would like to cultivate and how you can begin to experience that now.

My Greenhouse

I want to cultivate (core value):

How I can create that now:

Examples:

My Greenhouse:

I want to cultivate (core value): *Optimism*

How I want to feel: *Hopeful, happy, encouraged*

How I can create that now: *I will acknowledge the good with the bad: for every negative thing I say, I will end it with a positive: "I felt like a failure when I burned dinner, but it turned into a fun opportunity for a spontaneous pizza night full of laughter and connection."*

My Greenhouse:

I want to cultivate (core value) : *Ambition*

How I want to feel: *Excited, confident, Satisfied*

How I can create that now: *I will involve my children in my passion for photography by taking them on photo walks in nature or capturing candid moments at home. This will allow me to bond with my children while also pursuing my creative interests and building my photography skills.*

My Greenhouse:

I want to cultivate (core value): *Lifelong learning*

How I want to feel: *Patient, curious, proud*

How I can create that now: *I will reflect each Sunday on a rose-bud-thorn in my current stage of motherhood.*

As we cultivate our goals and values, it's important to regularly reflect on our progress and experiences. One effective method is using the rose-bud-thorn framework, which helps us appreciate our successes, recognize areas of growth, and acknowledge the challenges we face. This reflection process allows us to stay connected to our core values and continually nurture our identity flowers. Notice how I applied this here.

Rose:

One thing that's going really well is the bedtime routine with my toddler. We've <u>learned</u> how to establish a calming and consistent routine that helps him fall asleep quickly and sleep through the night. It's been wonderful to have peaceful evenings and a well-rested child.

Bud:

I'm <u>learning</u> more about gentle parenting techniques. It's a new approach for me, and I'm seeing positive changes in my child's behavior and our relationship. It's encouraging to see how understanding and empathy can make such a difference.

Thorn:

One thing that's really challenging right now is managing my time. Balancing work and household responsibilities and spending quality time with my kids is tough. I often feel stretched too thin and struggle to find time for myself. I <u>want to learn</u> more about soul-care this week and how to be more intentional in filling my cup first.

Take a minute to fill out your greenhouse.

My Greenhouse:

I want to cultivate (core value):_____

How I want to feel:

_____

_____

_____

How I can create that now:

_____

_____

_____

As you journey through the process of nurturing your goals and dreams, remember that creating a greenhouse for your identity flowers is essential. This greenhouse is a space where you can protect and foster your aspirations, free from the distractions and challenges of the outside world. It's a place where you can truly be yourself, grow, and thrive.

In this nurturing environment, you have the freedom to focus on what matters most to you. By setting clear intentions and creating structured spaces for your goals, you allow them to flourish. Whether it's through optimism, lifelong learning, ambition, or any other core value, your greenhouse is where your identity can expand and blossom.

By regularly tending to your greenhouse, you ensure that your goals and dreams are always given the care and attention they need. Your greenhouse is a sanctuary for your aspirations, a place where you can continually cultivate and harvest the beautiful identity flowers that make up your unique self.

Embrace this journey of growth and transformation. Allow yourself to dream, to cultivate, and to thrive. Your greenhouse is waiting, and the possibilities are endless. **You are allowed to be a mother AND have dreams.**

Bloom Tip:

Create a dedicated space in your life—a "greenhouse"—where you can nurture and protect your dreams and goals. Regularly tend to this space by removing distractions and setting clear intentions, allowing your unique identity flowers to thrive.

SIX
BLOOM BEYOND:
Fertilizer

(Achieving Balance)

"Ideals are like the stars—we [may] never reach them, but like the mariners on the sea, we chart our course by them."[15]

—**Carl Shurz**

---

[15] Carl Shurz quoted by then President Ronald Reagan, Toasts at the State Dinner for Chancellor Helmut Kohl of The Federal Republic of Germany, October 21, 1986, https://www.presidency.ucsb.edu/documents/toasts-the-state-dinner-for-chancellor-helmut-kohl-the-federal-republic-germany.

I remember walking into a friend's open-concept kitchen-dining-living room area. The smell of warm comfort foods wafted in the air, and I immediately felt taken care of. I placed my miniature crockpot on the counter with the other soups and felt a twinge of embarrassment as I compared my rubbery, emulsified cheese goop (loosely resembling broccoli cheddar soup) to the other grandiose concoctions. In a seemingly other life (pre-baby), I enjoyed cooking and was typically able to pull off recipes, but in my current state—sleep-deprived, overwhelmed, and exhausted—I hadn't been able to do it.

I was one day deep into two days of parent-teacher conferences, still adjusting to being back at work while having an infant at home, and so tired I could hardly think. My baby was experiencing a so-called sleep "progression" (learning to sleep like adults do), and I had spent nearly the entire night awake with him. Still, I was here at a friend's house gathering with several other women.

I had been diagnosed with postpartum depression and was making the effort to get out and socialize instead of spending another night binge-watching TV and eating a TV dinner consisting of cheese and crackers. While several people had reached out initially right after I had the baby, I now found myself isolated, agitated, and helpless at the conclusion of the fourth trimester.

I sat down at the table with my baby on my lap, since Dad was taking night classes in law school and we had no money for babysitters. Lately, no one had been offering to hold my baby, my house was in a wildly unnatural state, and I wanted to be rescued; you can't help yourself when you're in survival mode.

However, this time, the host immediately took my baby from me and started to make baby noises at him. Another woman asked me how I was doing and stared genuinely into my eyes, seeing all of me. She shared actionable tips for how she made it through sleep retraining, instead of spewing out generically trite responses such as, "Yeah, that sounds hard" or "I'm sorry you're experiencing that." I felt so held in that moment.

My days were packed to the brim, but it was as if I were a camel grazing on only straw all day. Sure, I was full, but I wasn't nourished. My team of teachers had been excited for me and very supportive while I was pregnant and teaching during my first year. Unfortunately, their perspective moved to judgment after I had the baby and was no longer "carrying my weight" on the team. They'd had so much advice and encouragement before I had the baby, but all of that evaporated afterward. I had befriended a new teacher on the team, whom the rest of the team also disapproved of, so I was thereby more disliked by association. This intensified my feelings that no one was in my corner. No one understood what it was like to be me at that moment. I was spiraling further down the cycle of shame, blame, guilt, and remorse.

These get-togethers in my neighborhood continued once every month after that, and I knew who to gravitate toward for help. That initial dinner became a defining moment in my motherhood. I learned who I could turn to in hard moments, who was going to truly listen, and who would be willing to hold or care for my baby with no strings attached. I continued to make efforts to get out of the house, even if it was a walk down the street instead of just to the mailbox. The days started to get lighter (both physically and metaphorically), I started medication for postpartum depression, and I formed a new normal with my team at school. I didn't turn to them for my problems because each time I was met with criticism for how I'd handled the situation. Instead, I rallied with the new teacher and other friends who truly had my back.

I learned of a woman who lived across the street from the school and provided childcare in her home for only the children of teachers. Another neighbor who was missing the baby phase offered to watch my son every Monday. I was finding support, love, and care in my village. I began engaging in activities that I hadn't been doing prior to having the baby. I rekindled the joy of creating for the sake of creating by learning how to paint on canvas with acrylics. I honed my baking skills by perfecting the best cinnamon rolls. I got back into running and would do Zumba with my new teacher friend in her classroom after school. This period in my life enhanced my ability to adapt to changes and navigate through various life stages and transitions.

Having multiple facets to your identity makes you more resilient in the face of challenges, as you can draw strength and perspective from different areas of your life. Life can be all-consuming, suffocating at times, *if we let it.* Choosing to have multiple identifiers, instead of only one identifier, helps us be multi-dimensional and maintain our identity.

I found that when I allowed myself to be multidimensional, I was able to own my true identity. I believe that once an identity flower has sprouted, we are ready to expand our garden. Incorporating fertilizer is important in this phase because it will help supplement nutrients that may have been depleted from the soil. However, too much fertilizer—or the incorrect mixture—will damage or kill the plant, so balance is critical.

Exploring identities beyond a singular role—such as motherhood or a career—can bring more balance into our lives. Taken to the extreme, though, and neglecting other areas of our life won't be good for us either, just like the incorrect mixture of or adding too much fertilizer. Unbalanced fertilizer can burn plant roots, cause stunted growth, and affect the overall health of the flower.

Everything is an exchange of energy. Money, which represents what you value, is an exchange of energy. You spend and you receive, but you must have the money first (from working, from a gift, from a family member, etc.) before it can go anywhere. When interactions have an even energy exchange, balance is achieved. However, a mismatch in energy leads to feelings of negativity. If you begin your day with your cup depleted, you won't have the energy to give. People are natural takers, driven by an instinct for survival. It is normal to feel resentment, bitterness, and frustration when the energy isn't aligned. As mothers, we give so much energy 24-7. So, how can you fill your cup to match the energy taken? We give and give to others expecting them to give back the same amount of energy, but they won't—that's not the deal. It is your responsibility to give to yourself to match the level of energy you are giving to others each day.

What kind of energy are you applying to life—what energy are you bringing to your family and society? If you currently feel "small," you'll bring resentment, bitterness, and envy into your day. If you feel "expansion," you'll bring light, joy, and relief with you.

Someone who feels small views time as scarce; she has numerous plans, dreams, and aspirations but no time to pursue them. Although she spends plenty of time with her children or giving to others, her time is dedicated to different activities. When she focuses on the lack of time for herself, her focus amplifies her sense of limitation.

Someone who finds expansion in motherhood feels invigorated and ready to start the day. She views time as abundant and allocates time for her plans, dreams, and aspirations, preventing feelings of being burdened by her children or others when spending time with them. Everything is well-compartmentalized.

Bloom Tip:

> "When you change your energy, you change your life."[16]

If you're always the giver, you'll feel depleted. If there's no energy coming in, yet you're putting energy out, you'll feel empty and exhausted.

MomSquad Secret

I was talking to a woman who is about ten years older than me. I told her I put my boys in daycare once a week to feel more

---

[16] Joe Dispenza, caption for post on Instagram (@drjoedispenza), October 21, 2020, https://www.instagram.com/drjoedispenza/p/CGn4ZbTnOSn/.

balance in my life, even though I am mostly a "stay-at-home mom." She said, "I wish that was socially acceptable when I was a young mom." We've all heard it takes a village to raise a child, but in modern American culture, we've moved away from involving outside hands and wear it as a badge of honor to do it all ourselves, and do it well. We weren't meant to parent in isolation. You were not meant to do this alone. You need support, and that doesn't make you weak—it makes you a mother.

When my boys are in daycare, they are being nurtured, just by someone else. It can be exhausting to always nurture! How can you miss your kids if they are never gone? When I pick them up, I *want* to be with them again. I've had enough space to breathe on my own that I can fully be present again—without the glazed-over eyes and agitated nervous system. It's so unhealthy to be buried day after day, week after week, layering on bitterness, resentment, and discontent. I have learned—and allowed myself—to ask for support, pay for support, and honor the needs I have so I can show up and be the best possible mom for my children and also be the woman I know I am here to be.

We know that the physical, mental, and emotional are all interconnected. Negative emotions are toxic in the body when they are not released. You may experience emotions such as emptiness, rage, or resentment. We need to recover as we go. Recovery is everywhere: athletes know that recovery is just as important as strength training; employees aren't expected to work 24-7; students aren't in school day and night. Many areas of life have mandatory recovery, but not day-to-day *being* or *mothering*. This includes recovering physically, mentally, and emotionally. Even "precovery" before an especially demanding day will pay off.

When we don't do the necessary healing work, we remain in a cave of poison. A healthy environment will eradicate weeds, but an environment left unchecked will choke beautiful flowers. We need to be aware of the areas in life where the unbalanced fertilizer has crept in. Can you or do you "take a break" from living or mothering? *You're allowed to.*

You are allowed to.

Many times people think that if they have dreams OUTSIDE of a designated role, it is selfish. I know that for many mothers, all they dreamed of was becoming a mother. So once they become a mother, they stop dreaming.

It is a tragedy for a human to stop dreaming. The minute we stop dreaming, we fall into "going through the motions." Life becomes rote and stagnant. Dreaming is integral to the human experience and to development; it fuels ambition, builds resilience, and encourages people to push beyond their current limits. When our lives lack dreams, they lack vitality, happiness, and the thrill of facing challenges. The forfeiture of these invaluable aspects of life lead to a diminished existence both individually and collectively.

You are allowed to dream.

We're so conditioned into playing it safe that we forget what it's like to dream big. Do you know how to dream? Fully unleash the confines and release inhibitions? "Make your dreams two sizes too big so you can grow into them."[17]

Some mothers are completely and wholly fulfilled by motherhood alone. In fact, they are thriving in it, while other mothers are not living in alignment because a lot of what fills them up is outside of motherhood. Every mother has her own strengths and talents. Each one is unique and perfect for her and her life. Not one mother is the same as another, yet we compare ourselves to the mothers around us as if we are equals. Imagine bringing your gardening gloves, trowel, watering can, and wheelbarrow to a court of law. Those tools are perfect for gardening, not being an attorney. Your tools might be different from another mother's. Some mothers' tools lend well to being a homemaker and nurturing children, while other mothers' tools support them working outside of the home while also mothering. Whatever tools you have been gifted with, you are capable of doing both—being a mother AND pursuing your passions *alongside motherhood.*

What's a dream you have deleted? Think back to your childhood self. Oftentimes, what we enjoyed as children we still enjoy as adults. Are your dreams hidden in a corner and gathering dust? Are there things you need to bring down from the shelf and incorporate back into your life? We are the ones who control the majority of our future with the energy we are currently bringing to our lives. You get to dictate where your life is headed. You get to apply the fertilizer.

---

[17] Quote the author recalls hearing while in attendance at a Religion in Life devotional at Utah State University. Exact date and specific speaker unknown.

Take a minute to remember a dream you deleted.

What is a dream I have deleted, forgotten, or ignored?

_____

_____

_____

_____

MomSquad Secret

A time in my life that I added too much fertilizer was when I hit my stress ceiling. I wasn't specifically looking for it, but once I was in the middle of it, I felt it. I was locked into several commitments outside the home, juggling many projects, had a few different deadlines, and was doing little to no soul-care. I hardly ever saw my children, was neglecting housework, and my body felt so weary; stress was literally taking the breath out of me. Thankfully, it was a temporary situation, and I did the excruciating work to cut things out and come back down so I could extract myself from the chaos. I had to start saying "no" more often, even though I didn't want to. Most of the time, it's not choosing between the good and the bad, it's choosing between the good and the good. It's hard to say no when it's something you care about, but it's critical for creating the life you want.

Some religious leaders have been known to encourage women to gain an education as "a backup plan." What if it wasn't a backup at all? *What if women sought higher education as a way to feel personally fulfilled?*

Also . . . just because you're working outside the home doesn't automatically mean you're fulfilled. There are a lot of women who are holding both: a career and the role of mother. I've heard of women who are so excited to leave the corporate world and transition into being a full-time stay-at-home mom. I was a teacher and a mom, and I wasn't fulfilled.

I see women decide to go back to school and pursue their education. They probably aren't in fulfillment during this time (unless school is fulfilling for them), but they are on the path toward it. I heard of an influencer who was on a path to decreasing her work to two hours a day. I loved the specificity of it. She named what she wanted and was taking steps toward it.

Many women have a clouded vision of who they are because their lives are so intertwined with their children; it's all muddled. Picture a Venn Diagram with three distinct sections: you, your children, the middle. When we have the areas clearly defined, we can see where possibility lies. Where are you spending the majority of your time? Are you putting fertilizer on only one group of flowers?

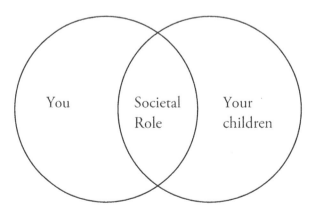

I had a career as a teacher while pregnant with my first child and taught until he was two.

I started my podcast less than a month before my second child was born. I made a commitment to release one episode every single week, and I have stuck to it.

I have been in active pursuit of my goals, regardless of what's going on around me. I hired a personal trainer six months after having my second baby and lost fifty pounds. I knew I was going to have more children, but I didn't use that as an excuse to put off getting in shape.

MomSquad Secret

Go back to your values. Is there an area you could outsource something that's lower on your values list? If you value quality time over thrift, could you hire a house cleaner to come once a month? —Ingrid

---

It is also important to note the reasons you're pursuing goals. Do you feel the need to prove your accomplishments to someone or even to yourself?

Basing one's worth on accomplishments can stem from various psychological, social, and cultural factors.

1. **Societal expectations:** Society often values success, productivity, and tangible achievements, which can lead individuals to measure their self-worth by their accomplishments.

2. **Parental influence:** Parents who emphasize achievement and success can instill these values in their children, making their children equate their worth with their performance and accomplishments.

3. **Comparison and social media:** Constant comparison with others, especially on social media where people often showcase their achievements, can lead individuals to feel that their worth is tied to what they accomplish.

4. **Perfectionism:** Perfectionists often believe that their value is tied to their ability to achieve high standards and succeed in their endeavors.

5. **Validation and approval:** Receiving praise and recognition for accomplishments can create a positive feedback loop where individuals seek more accomplishments to gain more validation and approval.

6. **Low self-esteem:** Those with low self-esteem may seek external achievements to compensate for their internal feelings of inadequacy.

7. **Cultural values:** Cultures that emphasize individual success and productivity over community and personal well-being can contribute to this mindset.

8. **Education system:** Schools and universities that prioritize grades, awards, and accomplishments can reinforce the idea that worth is tied to achievements.

Understanding these factors can help us recognize and potentially shift our perspective on self-worth.

Is it a stress response? Specifically "flight" in the fight-flight-freeze physiological response? Some people remain actively busy as a trauma response or coping mechanism.

I remember that I had a massage on my birthday one year and I shared with the therapist that I often carry my stress in my shoulders. She told me after the massage that she was talking with my spirit, asking why I was holding on so tight to this tension. The message she heard was that it was all I had ever known. Can we break old patterns and retrain our cells to unwind?

Does it come down to people-pleasing? Others overagree to commitments out of fear or as a way to fit in. Out of the following four personality types, I've recognized that a tendency in my personality is to be an obliger. Do you resonate with one of these?

> **Upholder**—accepts rules, whether from outside or inside. An upholder meets deadlines, follows doctor's orders, keeps a New Year's resolution.

> **Questioner**—questions rules and accepts them only if they make sense. They may choose to follow rules or not, according to their judgment.

> **Rebel**—flouts rules from outside or inside. They resist control. Give a rebel a rule, and the rebel will want to do the very opposite thing.

Obliger—accepts outside rules but doesn't like to adopt self-imposed rules.[18]

Or is it a genuine interest to pursue? As humans we are goal-oriented beings, but it's good to reflect on timing as fertilizer. Do you pursue your goals and dreams one at a time or all at once?

Imagine a garden where every setback is a stepping stone and every challenge a chance to grow. In this journey, your goals are your guiding stars. Even when the path seems daunting, remember that each obstacle is an opportunity to learn and become stronger.

 Embrace resilience. When faced with difficulties, don't be discouraged. Instead, see them as part of your unique story, adding depth and character to your journey.

 Find balance. It's essential to balance ambition with soul-care (the application of fertilizer). Take breaks, celebrate small victories, and nurture your well-being. A balanced approach keeps your spirit high and your mind clear.

 Stay focused. Keep your eyes on the prize, but be flexible in your methods. Adapt and innovate, and you'll find new ways to reach your goals, even when the original plan doesn't work out.

---

[18] Gretchen Rubin, "Four Personality Types: Which One Are You?" *The Happiness Project Blog*, January 7, 2013, https://gretchenrubin.com/articles/four-personality-types-which-one-are-you/.

Believe in you. Trust in your abilities and the process. With determination, patience, and a touch of belief, you can turn dreams into reality.

The quote, "if you're not happy single, you won't be happy taken" applies beyond relationships. If you feel like you're lacking in an area of life, it won't magically change by only altering your situation; you have to change your thoughts as well. Identity supersedes circumstances.

Our identity is rooted in core values and beliefs that are not easily swayed by external factors. While circumstances can be unpredictable and often beyond our control, our identity provides a stable foundation that guides our reactions and decisions. This intrinsic sense of self acts as an anchor, helping us navigate through life's ups and downs with resilience and clarity. By prioritizing our identity, we can maintain integrity and purpose, even when facing adversity.

To end this chapter, you will be writing a short biography for yourself as it reflects who you are today. By looking at this, you can observe (without judgment) the application of "fertilizer" in your life.

There is only one rule: don't include your children at all unless it's just a brief mention or at the end of it.

Biography Template

- Your name

- Things you love

- Skills you have (washing dishes, decorating, cooking, talking, sewing)

- Accomplishments (you could say: birthed 3+ kids, schooling, volunteer work—including school + church involvement)

- Something you are passionate about

I know how hard it is to write up a bio of yourself. It can be painful to look at the identity that we see for ourselves. I am inviting you to use Chat GPT to support you in writing YOUR biography.

Example (I put this into Chat GPT.)

Chat: Can you write me a bio?

My name is Jennifer Banks. My skills are reading, cleaning, gathering. My accomplishments are leading the women's group at church, birthing three kids, and participating in a ladies networking group. I am passionate about music.

Chat's response: Sure, here's a bio for you.

Jennifer Banks is a dedicated individual with a passion for music and a talent for organization. With a knack for reading, cleaning, and gathering, Jennifer's skills extend beyond the ordinary. She has been instrumental in leading the women's group at her local church, where she has demonstrated her leadership abilities and commitment to community. In addition to this, Jennifer is the proud mother of three children and an active participant in a ladies networking group. Her love for music fuels her creativity and brings joy to those around her. Jennifer is a shining example of someone who balances family, community, and personal interests with grace and determination.

Wow, isn't that amazing? Now, it's your turn! Type up this small portion of information and put it into Chat GPT. It's difficult for us to see ourselves clearly; we often need an outside perspective to understand our true selves.

> Name
> Things you love
> Skills
> Accomplishments
> Passions

MomSquad Secret

In the past, I have also taken the pursuit of my dreams to the extreme. I tend to have a lead foot, both in the car and in life. I often say yes without thinking as I work on my "invisible" bio and resume. However, awareness is over half of the solution. With a little bit of strategy and planning, we can achieve balance in our home and work lives. When it comes down to it, balance is a state of mind. Just like I knew when I hit my stress ceiling, you will too. Trust your intuition, rely on a higher power and others, and seek fulfillment—all in the right amounts of fertilizer for you.

Life can sometimes feel overwhelming and stifling if we allow it to. By embracing multiple identities instead of just one, we can become more multi-dimensional and preserve our sense of self. Once an identity flower has sprouted, we are ready to expand our garden. Just as plants need balanced fertilizer to thrive, we need to nourish our various roles and passions to maintain balance. Too much focus on one area can deplete the others, leading to resentment and burnout. By creating a nurturing, safe space for our goals and dreams, we allow each aspect of our identity to flourish, bringing more joy and fulfillment into our lives.

Bloom Tip:

Remember, your garden is *yours* to cultivate. Each identity flower you nurture adds depth and beauty to your life. Balance is key; too much focus on one area can deplete the rest. Embrace your multifaceted identity, and let each part of you bloom with purpose and passion. You are allowed to dream big and pursue your passions alongside motherhood or any other role you cherish. By fostering a supportive environment, you ensure that your entire garden thrives, and you become the greatest version of yourself.

SEVEN
BLOSSOM IN ADVERSITY:
Breaking the Seed Coat

(Surviving to Thriving)

"The flower that blooms in adversity is the most rare and beautiful of all."[19]

—Mulan

---

[19] *Mulan*, screenplay by Rita Hsiao, Chris Sanders, Philip LaZebnik, directed by Barry Cook, Walt Disney Feature Animation, released June 5, 1998 (USA).

Have you found that sometimes you expect to achieve your goals right away but are left feeling disappointed and frustrated when achieving them takes longer than you want? Do you wish it was easier, faster, or on YOUR own timeline? I find it interesting that perennials go through a wintering experience before blooming in the spring. They are able to withstand the cold, and they are able to survive for many growing seasons. We, too, need wintering experiences prerequisite for our growth. We go through so much to become so much.

"Stratification is the [wintering] process that a seed goes through to break down the seed coat and allow moisture to enter the seed to begin the germination process."[20] Many seed species have an embryonic dormancy phase and generally will not sprout until this dormancy is broken.

Just like the process of seeds germinating after wintering, our capacity for growth and expansion is increased with adversity. While I was in college, my parents got divorced. That was also the week I got married. It wasn't official that week, but that's when my mom told me it was her intention, so it was as good as done. I sobbed to my fiancé and asked if he still wanted to marry me despite my family issues. He said that he knew my family was part of the deal but that he was marrying me, not my parents. My dad wasn't mentally well enough to come to my wedding, so my older brother stood in for him.

---

[20] OPN Seed, "Learn about Stratification," https://www.opnseed.com/pages/learn-about-stratification (accessed July 26, 2024).

My husband consoled me many other times throughout the rest of that year as the divorce became finalized. I have learned that you can't dip your toes into the water and say you swam. You can't hide from adversity and say that you lived. You have to keep moving, keep going as you move toward healing. Just as we would never put a rubberband on a bud to prevent it from blooming, we damage our potential when we inhibit our growth. This experience during my engagement and wedding was a wintering phase for me. Little did I know that it was also my greatest growth time. Like the bulb under the earth, I was being prepared for all the blossoming ahead for me.

There are other experiences in our lives besides "wintering" that break periods of dormancy and allow us to crack open and start to bloom. These moments are called scarification. Scarification is when a seed is nicked or cracked to instigate breaking of the seed coat. This can happen in nature with animals or weathering but can also be mimicked by humans.

One of my scarification experiences has been navigating my adult relationship with my mother. Grief takes many forms. I've had to let go of the mother I always wanted so that I can accept the mother I have. Maybe there's a relationship in your life that isn't what you expected.

I have gotten to a point where I can meet her where she's at and not try to bring her up to where my needs are. Because I didn't have a deep connection with my mother while I was growing up, I sought out other mother figures. The focus is not about my relationship with mom; it's about **how I dealt** with my relationship with my mom and how I treat her now as a result.

I bet my mom felt confused and alone while raising my siblings and me. She went back to work as a way to cope with the difficulties of motherhood. I wonder how her motherhood would have been different had she had access to a book similar to this one.

While I was in college, I sent a card to my mother and included the following quote:

"I should never for a moment forget my duty towards my mother, she who has made me who I am and who will make what I will become, she who has spent the better portion of her life in my behalf and to whom I owe all the honor, respect, and affection that I can give."[21] — John A. Widtsoe

It's not easy to be a mom. I've seen that more and more as I've become a mother. God is the true parent and we have aptly been given the charge of apprentice as we clumsily walk the path of motherhood. Children come to earth with their own personalities. I am grateful for a mother who never gave up on me and put up with my stubborn attitude.

My mom and I have a much closer relationship now than we did when I was growing up and we were living in the same household. As we

---

[21] The author of this book copied this quote from an overhead transparency in a religion class at Utah State University and exhausted all efforts to find the original source and date of this quote from Widtsoe, without success.

give our children space to be themselves—instead of using force and coercion—we are more likely to attract them than repel them.

I see you. Maybe your adversity is a medically complex trial, infertility after initial success, loss of a loved one, getting laid off, moving away from family support . . . big events. This is the adversity I'm referring to. These are real, human experiences that we all have at one time or another, but maybe you're experiencing them right now *within motherhood*. **Suppression creates insanity.** We have to let it move through us; feelings buried alive never die. I believe emotional suppression causes physical problems. Allow yourself time to grieve.

After I had my first child, it took a long time to feel like myself again. It was almost an out-of-body experience where my mind and body felt disconnected, I didn't feel the same, and I was so **SO** sleep deprived. I had just finished my first year of teaching when I had my son, so I had the summer to experience matrescense. The second year of teaching—being a working mom—was extremely difficult. I developed postpartum depression a few months into the school year.

We lived away from family at the time, but I would write on the calendar when they were coming to visit. Having *something to look forward to* was so motivating that I began to write other little upcoming events on the calendar, too, even if it was something made up, such as *go get a fun drink*.

This reminds me of running. Even though it's hard at times, running is my exercise of choice. If I can just make it to the tree up ahead, I can keep going. If I can just make it to that sign, I can keep going. If I can just make it twenty feet, I can keep going. **Sometimes we try to see too far and we get discouraged.** The little mileposts along the way seem much more attainable. Focus just on the season you're in, or the day, the hour, or even the minute if you need to! No shame. No mom-guilt. *Sometimes we thrive and other times we just survive.*

Because it took a year to get pregnant the first time, we began trying for a second child around the time of my son's first birthday. There were many who told us it's faster after you've had one because your body knows what it's doing. We expected a fast conception, but it took nearly a year again. With our third, we accepted that it would take a slow year, so we tried a bit sooner. However, that time, it was fast— first try to be exact—so we ended up with children closer in age than we had anticipated. It seemed to be the opposite of what we expected each time. **Expectations can be harmful** when they are unrealistic, excessively demanding, or not aligned with one's abilities and situation.

Having two children so close together made me feel like I'd bitten off more than I could chew. It was the most difficult time in my motherhood. I felt trapped a lot of the time and adopted a victim mentality. The song "Big Love, Small Moments" by JJ Heller really helped me see the beauty in my circumstances.

> *Big magic in the mundane*
> *The big picture in a small frame*
> *Everything is sacred when you take time to notice*
> *Big love happens in the small moments.*[22]

---

[22] JJ Heller, "Big Love, Small Moments," single released January 4, 2019, Stone Table Records.

I'm in the process of deciding if I want a fourth child or not. When I voice this to others, some are confused. "I thought you didn't enjoy motherhood?" they ask. The early stages of motherhood were very trying for me, especially with children so close in age. However, I can see the big picture of my future family—my Thanksgiving table when they're all grown, the camaraderie and community we'll share—and that motivates me to continue building my family. I value community more than I mind the discomfort of the stage. One mentor encouraged me to write up two visions: one that includes a baby and one that doesn't.

MomSquad Secret

[Motherhood] is hard but rewarding. —Tami

Many studies have shown that pregnancy literally changes your brain so you can respond to the needs of your child. **You are equal to the task!** –Megan

---

Is there an outcome in your life you're holding onto? Maybe you could neutralize it by doing this practice. Write down two potential outcomes and compare them. Here are some examples to get you started.

One Thing I Desire	Potential Outcome #1	Potential Outcome #2
Business pursuit	Entrepreneurial path	Corporate career path
Gender contentment at birth	Baby boy	Baby girl
Moving	Relocating to a new city	Staying in my hometown
Education	Graduate work	Enter workforce
High quality of living	Buying a home	Continuing to rent
Growth & development	Starting/growing a family	Focusing only on personal goals
Job satisfaction	Changing careers	Advancing in current field
Traveling	International	Local or national
Lifestyle	Minimalist	Lavish
Income	Starting a side hustle	Committing fully to main job
Fulfillment	Community service	Prioritizing personal hobbies

You could even write out a third vision where applicable: a combination of the two outcomes and what that would look like. When you write out your potential outcomes (visions), **what emotions do you feel?** Do you find that it is hard for you to process emotions? I find that many mothers struggle to process emotions.

Mothers have excelled at showing up for their children because it is an instinct that has always been there. Mothers are not always the best at showing up for themselves alongside caregiving. We all know why Mama Bear's porridge was cold ;) There is room for both caring for children and caring for self. There **needs** to be both.

You are allowed to feel your feelings AND love being a mother, even if your feelings contradict the love you have for your children. There have been many times I've gotten stuck in a rut. As the oldest of two younger sisters and having babysat since age eleven, I'd already had a decade of mothering before I became a mother!

There has to be something (many things!) that light you up in addition to motherhood that help you expand.

I have found that through these simple exercises of processing my emotions, focusing on the next milepost, and managing my expectations, I have been able to move from surviving into thriving. But the truth is, it is only when I have gone through deep struggles that I have found my greatest reward. Can we really find joy in adversity? Do we have to just hold on and wait it out? We can find joy if we look for the tender moments—snapshots big and small.

I invite you to keep a journal. As you do so, consider writing one small, tender moment each time you write. One-line-a-day journals are perfect for this. You can also record these moments in the notes app on your phone, take a picture, or even just note them mentally in a moment of reflection. The point is to change the lens—over time—through which we are viewing motherhood.

Inherent Lens: This is our identity—who we truly are at our core. We were born with our worth intact and that worth does not increase or decrease over time.

Derived Lens: This is circumstantial—how we see ourselves changes based on who we're with and what's going on. We make situations mean something about us.

We're happiest and most aligned when we're using our inherent lens. It takes practice to view the world this way. As we notice which lens we're using, we can have a greater influence over how we're feeling. When we're using our inherent lens, we are internally in tune with leveraging our strengths, living our core values, nurturing our identity, watering our soul according to our needs and wants, and balancing our schedules and commitments so that we can authentically bloom.

When we're using our inherent lens, we can release the timeline: have children if and when **you** want them.

When we're using our inherent lens, we can release the shoulds: **you** are the mom your children need.

When we're using our inherent lens, we can release the mom-guilt: **you** are *equally* deserving of love and care.

When we're using our inherent lens, we can release the shame: you could only give 30% effort today and **you** *gave all the 30%* (or 100% of your available energy)!

When we're using our derived lens, we are focused on external sources and influences to tell us who we are and what we could be. We make circumstances and the opinions of others mean something (sometimes negative) about us. We're living our lives according to outward approval, making choices based on someone else's core values, putting up with tasks or situations that aren't our best fit, neglecting our needs and desires, staying dormant in our identity, and living an unbalanced schedule and life.

The main reason we do anything is for how we believe it will make us feel. Adversity is your fuel. When you are struggling, you aren't doing something wrong, you are growing. I wouldn't pray for my adversity-filled experiences, but I also wouldn't trade them. Everything I have experienced and felt has brought me to this current moment. My identity is fluid and each version of myself is stronger, more refined, and wiser than the last. The periods of wintering have made my blossoms all the more beautiful.

When life is going well, it's easy to forget about a Higher Power watching over us; we get complacent. It's especially in my adversities that I've relied on God. We would do well to involve Him in daily life and to "use [Him] as a steering wheel and not a spare tire."[23]

MomSquad Secret

Teach them the language of the spirit. —Irene

Life's adversities, much like the wintering process for perennials, are prerequisites for our growth and expansion. Just as seeds undergo stratification to break dormancy and begin germination, we, too, need to navigate life's challenges to unlock our potential. These experiences, whether they stem from personal struggles or significant life changes, allow us to break open, grow, and bloom. Embracing these periods of adversity with resilience and grace helps us develop a deeper, more multifaceted identity. By fostering a nurturing, safe space for our goals and dreams, we ensure that our identity flowers can thrive, bringing more joy and fulfillment into our lives.

As we cultivate our gardens, it is crucial to recognize the balance between our roles and passions. Exploring identities beyond a singular focus, such as motherhood *or* career, allows us to maintain a healthy and vibrant life. By embracing our inherent worth, focusing on our strengths, and nurturing our passions, we create an environment where we can bloom fully. Remember, your identity is fluid, and each version of yourself becomes stronger and more beautiful through the trials and

---

[23] Corrie ten Boom with Elizabeth and John Sherrill, *The Hiding Place*, (Bloomington: Chosen Books, 1971), original quote: "Use prayer as a steering wheel and not a spare tire."

triumphs you encounter. Embrace your multifaceted self, and let each part of you bloom with purpose and passion.

Bloom Tip:

> Select a few quotes that are personally meaningful to you for when you are facing adversity.

Impactful Quotes:

_____

_____

_____

_____

_____

_____

_____

_____

_____

_____

_____

_____

_____

_____

_____

_____

_____

_____

EIGHT
FROM WEEDS TO FLOWERS:

Pulling Weeds,

Pinching Flowers

(Changing Limiting Beliefs)

"What you dislike in another take care to correct in yourself."

—Thomas Sprat
(widely attributed, original source unknown)

Pinching and weeding are two similar techniques in which you cut parts of plants to help promote growth. Pinching involves removing a portion of a plant to encourage additional growth. It seems like it would harm the plant, but really it's allowing it to grow even bigger than it would have before; it allows it to expand.

Weeding is also fundamental for a garden to reach its full potential. Have you ever gone to your garden only to see that the whole garden bed was taken over with weeds, seemingly overnight? Oftentimes, we don't notice the weeds in our lives until they have overtaken our minds completely. The weeds often arise slowly and then take over without our consent. I want to help you weed out what is hindering your growth so you can live your most fulfilled life. Weeds are noxious; they take up space and also take nutrients from other plants.

Is it time to pinch some of your flowers? Is it time to pull out some weeds? Just look at a woman and all she can do in a home setting. She multi-tasks like nobody's business, sometimes even with a baby on her hip. Just imagine what she could do with space! Don't be afraid to pinch or weed some of your current beliefs. You are so capable!

While pinching encourages healthy growth, it's also essential to address the less desirable elements in your garden. Just as plants benefit from pinching and weeding, your life will benefit from expansion and from removing the weeds that hinder your growth. Different situations will require a little or a lot of pinching and weeding. If you only pinch a weed, or if it's not detached from the ground entirely, it will grow back. For more invasive weeds, we need to pull them out at their roots to ensure their removal. Let's look at some weeds that may be getting in the way and some flowers we can pinch to help you step into your full identity.

Bloom Tip:

> **This season is not forever.** The hard things won't last forever; you can get through them. The joyful things won't last forever. Enjoy them. —Mandy

From Weeds to Flowers: Fear & Possibility

Pulling the weeds of fear

There are many voices that ask, "What about the *children*?" But what about **YOU**? Nobody asks about you. Mothers have been neglected along the way for generations!

Fear is a window into our deepest desires. Are you afraid you won't be a "good mom" if you set some "selfish" goals? You can AND *need* to hold both. You can be a mess AND amazing. You can be proud of where you're at AND humble enough to learn more. You can care for your children AND chase your dreams. You can be content with your life AND want more. You are valuable AND a work in progress. There is no all-or-nothing.

Are you afraid of leaving your children in the care of another for a time? If so, is it for physical reasons or emotional reasons? Understanding these fears and addressing them through planning, finding reliable caregivers, and gradually increasing the duration of separation can help you feel more comfortable leaving your children.

Many times we are afraid of others' judgments. We think, "they'll like me if . . ."

Remember, we come to earth uniquely our own. From the day we are aware of our surroundings, we begin to assimilate "shoulds" and develop societal programming. We continue this practice until we gain self-awareness and then begin the process of untangling the mess to come back to the view of our self.

Self - Should - Self

Self   Should   Self

MomSquad Secret

Mind your own motherhood. Find the peace and joy within your own abilities, surroundings, and actions. —Becca

---

We are especially afraid of the judgment of family members. We were raised a certain way and when we stray from that, it shakes things up.

People like to keep us safe in the boxes of who they remember us to be. It can feel like we're not allowed to grow and evolve.

This fear of judgment can also extend to our most intimate relationships, such as those with our significant others. We fear how changes in ourselves might affect our partners, or how we will navigate the evolution of our identities together.

> "A successful marriage requires falling in love many times, always with the same person."[24]
> **—Mignon McLaughlin**

I think this is why the divorce rate is so high—two people change, but not together. Or, in ways that the other can't reconcile. This applies to ourselves as well. We are always changing into the next iteration of ourselves. But we don't allow ourselves to get the support we need in our transformations.

Sometimes we grow without considering whether or not we are growing together. If one partner grows excessively and at the expense of the other, it can become like an invasive species. However, when growth is complementary, it forms a symbiotic relationship.

When we neglect self-development and growth we risk turning our worst fears into reality. By not investing in ourselves we often find that the very things we feared come to pass because we haven't equipped ourselves to handle the changes and challenges.

---

[24] Mignon McLaughlin, *The Second Neurotic's Notebook*, (Indianapolis: Bobbs-Merrill, 1966).

Maybe you're counting the cost or effort involved in self-development. The fear of investing in ourselves can hold us back, but it's crucial to recognize the importance of seeking support and growth. When I was growing up, I babysat a lot. My biggest fear in parenthood was the 24-7, around-the-clock care. I brought that fear into my journey as a mom. I brought the shackles along as a self-fulfilling prophecy.

MomSquad Secret

Don't worry about things that won't matter in a week. Fear likes to take over. Take three deep breaths and ask yourself if the situation at hand will truly matter in time. If it will, seek resources and support. If it won't, let it go. —Amber

---

Other times, we fear the changes success may bring. As Marianne Williamson wrote,

> Our deepest fear is not that we are inadequate. Our deepest fear is that we are powerful beyond measure. It is our light, not our darkness that most frightens us. We ask ourselves, Who am I to be brilliant, gorgeous, talented, fabulous? Actually, who are you not to be? You are a child of God. Your playing small does not serve the world. There is nothing enlightened about shrinking so that other people won't feel insecure around you. We are all meant to shine, as children do. We were born to make manifest the glory of God that is within us. It's not just in some of us; it is in everyone and as we let our own light shine, we unconsciously give

other people permission to do the same. As we are liberated from our own fear, our presence automatically liberates others.[25]

Pinching the flowers of possibility

Instead of remaining inside the room of fear, keep the door of possibility open. There will never be a time that "you've arrived" or have reached your full potential. We are capable of infinitely more and should thereby wear out our lives in that pursuit.

> How often we are admonished not to waste time. What an absurdity. We can't waste time, or spend it, or save it. It is like warning a fish in the ocean not to waste water. We have no influence at all on time, any more than we have on space. We are born in it; it surrounds us all. What we can–and do–waste is ourselves. The personal tragedy–the waste–lies in what we do not give, the efforts we do not make, the powers we do not use, the happiness we do not earn, the kindness we neglect to bestow, the noble thought and deeds that could be ours if only we realized why we are here. You say you are wasting time. Correct yourself. Say, frankly; "I am wasting me."[26]
>
> **—Guideposts May 1959**

---

[25] Marianne Williamson, *A Return to Love: Reflections on the Principles of "A Course in Miracles,"*, (New York: HarperCollins, 1992).
[26] The author of this book copied this quote from an overhead transparency in a religion class at Utah State University and exhausted all efforts to find the original source and date of this quote from Guideposts but because of the date, there is no online version to consult or verify.

Are you wasting you? You live in the story that you don't have enough time. You've been conditioned to hurry up, make the most of it, and soak in every second with your children. But when you say yes to something, you're saying no to something else. What if you made a plan to attend X number of games, practices, or activities instead of every single one? Carve out space for you to grow because you're gardening all day anyway. Make a plan and then don't back down. Sometimes, we have to get creative. What if you used a two-hour childcare time slot at a gym and worked out for a half hour, then used the rest of the time to work on a project before picking them up? You have not failed if you have tried.

In the book *The 100 Years of Lenni and Margot*, Lenni is a fifteen-year-old with cancer. She asks a pastor, "Why am I dying?" After giving it some thought, the pastor replies, "Why are you living?"[27]

Living authentically means embracing both growth and change, much like the plants in a garden do. By pinching away the beliefs and fears that no longer serve us, we create room for new possibilities to flourish. Imagine your potential if you gave yourself permission to grow beyond the roles that confine you. Don't let the fear of judgment or failure prevent you from pursuing your dreams. Every time you say yes to personal growth, you say yes to a more vibrant and fulfilling life. This isn't about neglecting your responsibilities; it's about recognizing that you are just as important as the tasks and people you care for. You are

---

[27] Marianne Cronin, *The One Hundred Years of Lenni and Margot*, (New York: Harper Perennial, 2021).

capable of incredible things, and it's time to step into that potential with confidence.

Remember, true living involves continually stretching beyond our comfort zones and expanding our horizons. When we invest in self-development, we transform our lives and create a ripple effect that touches everyone around us. The fears that once seemed insurmountable become stepping stones to greater achievements. Make a plan, carve out space for your growth, and don't back down. As the pastor from *The 100 Years of Lenni and Margot* poignantly asks, "Why are you living?" Let this question drive you to live purposefully, embracing every opportunity to grow and bloom. Your life is your garden, and it's time to cultivate it with intentionality and passion.

From Weeds to Flowers: *Guilt & Intention*

Watering the weeds of guilt

I hear women talk about "mom guilt." These feelings often arise from the internal and external pressures to meet high standards of motherhood, balance work and family life, and fulfill societal expectations. Guilt, like fear, is just a weed that's growing. It's a window into a need or desire. I rarely have mom guilt; I know my children are getting the care they need and having the necessary experiences for growth. What I do experience more often, however, is spouse guilt. This is a window into how I wish my husband would care for and help me.

After my husband and I had been married for a year, the newlywed love began to fade a bit. We were still obsessed with each other, but it turned more into a practical sort of love. I had Jared read about the five love languages and we determined that his highest modes of receiving love were quality time and acts of service. Mine were words of affirmation and gift giving.

I tend to show love the way I receive it, so I always made sure to leave him little notes and gifts in his sock drawer, on the milk jug, by his pillow—the whole nine yards. He very rarely reciprocated because he showed love the way he received it—spending time with me on a date or vacuuming the living room.

I had heard my whole life that a man would complete me; he would be my other half. I had also internalized that both of you bring 100% to the relationship. I began keeping score, noting how much I did compared to him, how often I poured out my love and how infrequently he did (from my perspective with how I interpret love). I began to feel more and more empty.

I read about the "love tank" in the book *The 5 Love Languages*[28] by Gary Chapman and decided to make a paper representation of how depleted I felt at any given time. I made it look like a gas tank gauge, complete with an arrow fastened with a brad to indicate empty or full. I colored it and taped it right above our light switch. Look how helpful I was being! I could help my husband *see* when I needed some extra love.

---

[28] Gary Chapman, *The 5 Love Languages: The Secret to Love that Lasts*, (Chicago: Northfield, 1992).

Unfortunately, it had the opposite effect. Who knew? My husband saw it as a way for me to control him, and I ended up feeling more alone in my marriage than ever. We hear that communication is important, but we're never shown *how* to communicate. After wallowing in self-pity for a time, I pulled up my pants and got to work meeting my own needs.

I found that it was so much easier that way! I knew exactly what I needed, in exactly the right way, at the right time. I began buying myself gifts, purchasing fresh flowers, going out with friends, hosting get-togethers . . . it was a dream! My cup was the fullest it had ever been.

I fell into a pattern of independently getting what I wanted and went on that way for a long time. I began to expect that he couldn't meet my needs and I relied only on myself. In doing this, I started to sever my connection to him and build a wall in our relationship. At the time, I didn't even see this. I wasn't aware that by removing him from the equation, I was rendering him entirely useless to me.

I shared with a mentor how good I'd gotten at getting everything I needed. I told her about my upcoming plans to book a trip for my birthday. She reminded me to give my husband the opportunity to assist in fulfilling my desires. That was a wake-up call. All of a sudden, I could see how I had cut him out. By meeting every single one of my needs alone, I was denying him the opportunity of even helping in the process.

I saw the times that I had bought myself flowers for the morning of Valentine's Day, only to realize that he had bought a bouquet on his way home from work in the evening. I had gotten babysitters without even consulting his plans and availability first. I had preemptively bought a used laptop three weeks before my birthday only to learn that my husband had plans to order me a brand new one as a gift.

We know there is danger in the extremes. I had entered marriage with the expectation that he would meet every one of my needs. I had then shifted my belief by owning all of the responsibility to meet my own needs. When the pendulum is at either of the two ends, there is suffering. It is only in the middle that we can find healing and love. By voicing and naming our desires, we see what's possible and then we can come together and find a beautiful balance in how to meet them.

I used to feel a lot of spouse guilt when I would participate in social activities outside of the home in the evenings. I craved and needed connection with others, but I would feel bad that my husband had to do bedtime routines with the children after a long day of work. A friend pointed out to me that I had also had a long day of work (with the children) and that it was healthy to take turns with "the second shift." My husband and I came to a decision that he would take care of bedtime a couple nights of the week. I would take the other nights but request help when needed. It helped to know that I could count on those days, at a minimum, guilt-free.

Where are you in having your needs met? Are you on either side of the pendulum? Somewhere in the middle?

Partner meets all of your needs:

You never have to lift a finger and want for nothing. He/She tells you constantly how wonderful you are and how much you mean to him/her, buys you lavish gifts, writes love notes, and gives you small tokens of appreciation. He/She can't keep his/her hands off you and envelopes you in warm embraces—he/she satisfies your libido. He/She does everything around the house and cooks all of the meals. He/She works a full-time job and cares for the children. If it sounds like a fairytale, it's because this is what a lot of us saw in the media.

You meet all of your partner's needs:

He/She never has to lift a finger and wants for nothing. You tell him/her constantly you're with an exceptional individual. You buy him/her gifts, write love notes, and give him/her small tokens of appreciation. You encourage him/her and support his/her dreams. You don't always want sex, but you comply when he/she asks. You do everything around the house and cook all of the meals. You care for the children daily, including taking them to appointments, activities, and school. You do their bedtime routines at night so your partner can relax after a day of work. You give without expecting anything in return but then wonder why you're filled with resentment.

You meet all of your own needs and/or your partner meets all of their own needs:

You are a hard worker and you make things happen. You could live on the money you alone bring in. You don't need anyone's approval and are confident in who you are. You obtain all of the things you need and want. You meet your own sexual needs. You are aware of the tasks that need doing and take them upon yourself. You are tending to your physical, mental, and emotional needs by making all of the appointments and paying all the bills. Care of the children is solely your charge.

Meet in the middle to meet both of your needs:

There is a division of labor in household tasks. You rely on the income of both partners or recognize that one is working outside the home and one is working inside the home. Each partner expresses love and gratitude for the other in a variety of ways and levels. You ask for support, not permission, in goals or activities you want to pursue. Both of you come together for sexual fulfillment and are aware of how the other wants to interact physically. Both of you are tending to your physical, mental, and emotional needs, and you have a rhythm for scheduling appointments and paying bills. You are equal partners in caring for the children.

You can want that. You're allowed to create the life you want. If you want a happy ending, that only depends on where you stop your story.

There are times when the workload feels unbalanced, but I'd rather do the mental work (eliminating resentment) to be okay with the situation rather than trying to get it to be different by talking about it with my husband. I've gotten used to the "normal" and don't want to interrupt the flow of reality. It's hard for me to relinquish control. I prefer to be the full owner of creating the reality of my expectations.

1. Is it only *you* that wants something done? Or is it a common goal you share?

2. What is the feeling of keeping it the way it is? What is the feeling you'd gain if it were different?

3. What is the cost of changing it?

However, when we come together, we are bringing the pendulum back to the middle, rather than keeping it on either end of the extremes. When you're aware of each other's goals and expectations and you genuinely care when discussing plans, you'll be able to avoid feeling resentment when your needs aren't met. You can take care of your own needs, resent your partner for not meeting your needs, or come together with intention on how to meet each individual's needs.

MomSquad Secrets

A friend said guilt "just happens" for her. We can become so used to the habit that it feels automatic. But we learn from Viktor Frankl that this isn't the case:

"Between stimulus and response *there is a space*. In that space is *our power* to choose our response. In our *response* lies our growth and our freedom"[29] (emphasis added).

I was talking to someone who tried to motivate me in my parenting by saying, "You don't want to have regrets." This phrase kept coming back to me, and the more it did, the more I realized that I wasn't afraid of having regrets. I don't live my life that way. I believe that we're meant to have the experiences that we do, for better or for worse. There are lessons in all of it.

---

[29] Viktor Frankl, *Man's Search for Meaning*, (Boston: Beacon Press, English version, released 1959).

Pinching the flowers of intention

I'm good at living my life intentionally. When we make intentional choices, we're less likely to have guilt because there was a reason we made the choice initially. If we're comfortable and confident in making the decision, we can be comfortable and confident with the repercussions. We can be at peace with what comes.

One of the first inspirational quotes I remember being touched by was written below a picture of Jesus Christ. It said, "The greatest gift I could give to you is if you could see yourself the way I do." It hit me so hard and conveyed the magnitude of what I could become if I could change the way I viewed myself.

When we stay inside the seeds of who we are, we don't expand, crack open, and bloom. There are so many paths to growth. When we stay only on the path of motherhood, or a single role, our growth is stunted—restricted to one form of expansion. To open the channels of possibility, we have to walk other paths and be open to blooming.

MomSquad Secret

"You're not going to do it, are you?" "I don't think now is the right time . . . not while you have little kids at home." I've been met with these and other statements as I've pursued dreams as a mother. And while there are many arguments for both sides, I think now IS the perfect time to nurture my dreams *as* I nurture my children. Do children need love, care, and attention? Absolutely. Does it have to be me providing that for them 100%

of the time? Absolutely not. I was meant for more. You are meant for more.

I want my children to see my example of dedication to my dreams. When we elevate ourselves, our children have a higher starting point to jump from.

We've heard stories of women being told to stay in their lane, avoid risk, play small . . . this is happening in motherhood. Women use motherhood as a crutch: "I can't. I'm on mom duty." They let themselves dream once and when their fear comes to pass they say, "I tried that once; it didn't work." Mothers make excuses about what gets in the way. What the hell? How are we doing this to ourselves? How dare we use that as a crutch?

Growing up, I wasn't the most pleasant child to raise; I didn't take no for an answer. I know looking back I "gave" my mother a lot of grief. It's fascinating now to see how this has become my greatest super power: I make things happen, I don't back down, and I get what I want in life.

We all have our reasons for the choices we make. It's important to check in every so often and make sure that the reasons are serving us, creating the life that we want.

MomSquad Secret

Growing up, my absolute favorite dinner was "plate of little things." My single mom would slice cheese, apples, crackers, hot dogs, dry cereal, whatever and we would eat it in front of the TV.

I told her recently and she gasped, "What? Those were the nights I failed. I didn't cook a thing and was too tired to talk to you girls. That's ridiculous." Goes to show, **it may be JUST when we "fail" that our kids feel most happy.**" —Kimberly

From Weeds to Flowers: *Passivity* & *Belief*

Pulling the weeds of passivity

I see you. You're helping others shine. You fulfilled your roles, and now you sit back to watch your posterity do the same. You went to school, got married, had kids, and now you're done. Except you're not. You're living in *passivity*. You're hiding behind motherhood. You are numb.

I've been alive for thirty years but have only been awake, truly awake, for ten of those years. I met my first life coach when I was twenty and learned that there is a different way to do life. We can have a life full of abundance, choice, potential, and limitless beliefs.

The life coach "prescribed" me new beliefs to try on. One of the first ones I remember was, "I choose to enjoy this moment." I have employed this thought on numerous occasions when I'm in a less-than-ideal situation but still have the power of my mind. This has caused me to continually nourish the thoughts I'm having and cultivate a positive outlook.

There is so much to do, be, and see in this world we live in. We could spend every waking moment of our entire lives voraciously doing all the things and we would still barely scratch the surface. At some point in our lives, many of us stop talking about "what we want to be when we grow up." Some maintain an invisible but rigid boundary regarding what is and isn't possible to attain or become in life. You're fifty-three but feel that's too old to start piano lessons? Nonsense. You can still do, be, and see anything you want.

Regardless of what someone is experiencing, you can tell how they view the world by how they talk about it. Is their outlook positive or negative? Do they feel equipped with the resources to balance the demands placed on them? Tell me your opinion and you'll show me your mind.

When I was an elementary school teacher, we had an annual Walk to School Day in the fall. Parents and buses would drop children off at the far end of the street that the school was on, about a mile away, so they could walk or bike to school. Teachers who had agreed to participate would meet there, too, and join the students in the walk. The start time for school that day was delayed and after the walk there were refreshments in the faculty lounge for teachers and volunteers.

One year, there were two new teachers on my second-grade team. They heard about the Walk to School Day and asked me what it was. I told them about it in great detail and remarked that it was "soooo fun!" They joined me that year in participating and afterward I asked them what they thought. The teachers both said similar things: "It was okay" and "I wouldn't say that it was soooo fun." They didn't share my opinion. Life is truly what you make it; you get out what you put in.

I can see, too, how I may have hyped it up so much that they were imagining more. One of my favorite high school teachers would encourage us on each test day not to talk about the level of difficulty to our peers who would be taking the test on the following day (we had an A/B day schedule). The teacher said that if we portrayed the test as "hard," the other students might cram in extra study. If we portrayed it as "easy," they may have a false sense of unnecessary preparation and neglect to prepare as much as they need.

We can also project our negative feelings and/or trauma onto our children. If we've had bad experiences with the dentist or other fearful moments, we can potentially influence, for better or for worse, how our children view the situation when they encounter it.

Pinching the flowers of belief

We are also afraid because of our own limiting beliefs.

> *Who am I to do this?*
> *I'm not allowed to enjoy life in this way.*
> *I come last.*
> *Motherhood is meant to be hard and full of suffering.*

These fears make us tangled as if in rope. We are holding on so tight, waiting in bondage.

Some people fall over in this space. They are waiting, and they are angry—so, so angry. "Just fill me up," they plead. True fulfillment doesn't come from without; it comes from within. We saw this in the experience with my husband—my unmet needs caused bitterness and suffering. But until you walk away from it, you don't even realize it's there.

There are these two young fish swimming along and they happen to meet an older fish swimming the other way, who nods at them and says "Morning, boys. How's the water?" And the two young fish swim on for a bit, and then eventually one of them looks over at the other and goes "What the hell is water?"[30]

Recognizing the anger and bitterness for what they are then gives us leverage. Naming them removes their influence. No one blames a hummingbird for just filling herself up. Identify where and how you carry your anger and bitterness. Is it in clenched fists, tension headaches, or in the pit of your stomach?

Do you wake up excited and ready to face the day? Or are you filled with dread at the thought of "doing it all over again?" I knew it was time to leave teaching when it took so much motivation to get out of bed and face another day at school. If you are feeling dread, something is not aligned in your life.

Is that an area that's lacking in your life? Do you hold resentment toward others? Some women may feel bitter when their husbands leave

---

[30] David Foster Wallace, "This Is Water," May 21, 2005, commencement speech delivered at Kenyon College, Gamber, Ohio.

for work in the morning. The husband gets to contribute to society, be among coworkers, and have a nice lunch out, whereas the wife stays home surrounded by children, can't have adult conversations, and eats peanut butter and jelly sandwiches.

Resentment may also come from doom-scrolling on social media. Do you feel jealous when you see people posting about vacations, possessions, or other experiences? Resentment comes from envy.

Do you feel like motherhood is a life sentence? Do you spend your days watching shows and scrolling to pass the time? Pass the time to what? Death?! You're not in this forever. You're always a mother, but your seasons will change. Happiness isn't a single choice; it's the sum of many choices.

Are there weeds of mindless convention in your garden?

> *This is the way it's always been done.*
> *Mothers are meant to be at home with their children.*

Weeds of the compulsion to ask for permission? Who says what is and isn't allowed?

Perhaps you've noticed the weeds of *doubt*. Prior to writing this book, an individual asked me about my plans. I told him about my upcoming author adventure to write a book in a week and he said, "I don't mean this to come across offensively, but what are your credentials?" I was able to laugh off the question because doubt is not a weed that I let hang around. We can do anything we truly want to do.

I used to say that I became a teacher because my mom told me to. Recently, I realized that I don't want this to be my story anymore. I became a teacher because that was the way, the path I needed to be on to arrive where I currently am. We can fall victim to the circumstances we're in or we can take back the power to reclaim our identity.

The more we take ownership of our desires, the more power we have in creating that reality.

The first podcast I ever listened to was, *Better Than Happy* with Jody Moore. I started listening in 2019 after a member of my book club shared some advice she'd heard from Jody's podcast. Jody was another life coach I learned from. Her content was an incredible foundation heading into the COVID-19 pandemic. I listened to every episode she released, alternating between past episodes and new episodes until I was current. I have met her in person several times, she's been a guest on my podcast, and I've enrolled in many of her courses. Jody unveiled an in-person business school opportunity. I was immediately on board. Though it was a big chunk of money to invest, I signed up for the business school. Part of the offering for the business school was to be connected with Jody's children's book publisher, Keira Brinton.

A couple months prior to the start of business school, Jody ultimately decided to cancel it and she refunded the money. I was devastated. I was prepared to not forgive Jody for moving a different direction. However, Jody explained that she wanted to focus on her highest calling—improving the mental health of individuals—and she felt that business school was a distraction from that. I couldn't fault her for following her intuition. I asked Jody if I could still be connected with Keira and she linked us together via email.

Keira Brinton owns Joan of Arc Publishing—the publishing house that published this book that you're reading. I thought business school was the way to the next version of myself, but really it was the way to meet Keira and bring this book to life. Participating in an author adventure (writing a book in five days at a location away from home) cost three times more than business school. Each time I have invested money in myself, I have grown more confident in showing up and **allowing** myself to spend the money on me.

People tend to find fault like there's a reward for it, especially when it comes to criticizing themselves. It's as if we are holding a flower bouquet and pulling flowers out one by one: I love this attribute, I don't love this quality. I love you, I love you not . . .

Maybe you've heard these things too.

> *I hate my stomach.*
> *My arms are so flabby.*
> *She's so fit.*
> *Maybe if I was prettier, my husband would want me more.*
> *Maybe if I had different boobs or did my hair differently, I would be accepted.*

We have to stop talking to ourselves like this. These phrases are officially retired. The brain is so used to these neural pathways that if we don't give it different material to work with, it will fall back into old patterns.

My wedding ring no longer fits. Instead of saying, "I've gained weight," I can change it to, "The new shape that I've become requires a new wedding ring," and "my current body size requires some new underwear." How is it that we can love our children for who *they* are but not ourselves for who we are—our body, our hair, the wrinkles that are finding their way onto our faces.

Mantras that change our brains:

- I know there is no price tag to my dreams.
- I am the only one who can give my child a happy, fulfilled mother.
- I choose to enjoy this moment.
- I trust that my life is unfolding beautifully.
- I release all that doesn't serve me.
- I live the truth of who I am.
- I am not ashamed of my power.
- I am a divine feminist.
- I embody my soul's highest vibration.
- I do not back down.
- I am at peace with what comes and what goes.
- I relish the essence of my femininity.
- I am equally deserving of love and care.
- I receive the highest good.

- I trust my intuition.

- I live in alignment with my highest calling.

- I am fully unleashed.

- I reclaim my power.

- I defy convention.

- I, alone, am whole.

Why do we feel like we have to excuse ourselves? Sometimes we erroneously think, "If I just acknowledge it, I'm excused from the judgment." But we're still judging ourselves. That wears down our self-worth. We are whole just as we are. No one else is needed for us to be complete.

We do this with our cooking: "I'm sorry, I only had an hour to throw this together." We do this when we apologize for our children's negative behavior, as if their mood is a reflection of our parenting. Stop talking yourself down and downplaying who you are! God doesn't make mistakes.

Are you spending too much time on your outward appearance? There are many women who say they don't have "time" to pursue their goals, yet they spend half a day getting their hair done. Are you putting an equal amount of work into your mental and emotional selves? If you reduce the time you spend in a certain area, will you have more space to work on a goal?

Do you have a morning routine? Get sun on your face as soon as you get out of bed to stimulate the circadian rhythm and get you going. Then, if the rest of your morning routine is tailored for you, you'll start your day on much better footing. Maybe you can't do your morning routine first thing when you wake up because of your specific circumstances, but identify a time frame and length of routine that would work best in your current situation.

Morning routine

Get ready for the day before or after the routine.

Short (5 minutes or fewer)

- Mantra (1 minute)
  Find a cozy spot, such as a comfortable chair or a corner with soft cushions. Sit quietly and repeat a positive mantra like, "Today, I choose joy and positivity."

- Intention setting (1 minute)
  While in your cozy spot, take a deep breath and set an intention for the day. For example, "My intention today is to stay calm and focused."

- Journal (1 minute)
  Take out your journal and quickly jot down three things you're grateful for, a few thoughts on how you plan to achieve your intention, or a small, tender moment from the previous day.

- Movement (1 minute)
  Stand up and do a quick series of stretches or a brief yoga pose to wake up your body.

- Crystal roller (1 minute)
  Use your cold crystal roller (stored in the fridge) on your face, taking a moment to enjoy the calming sensation, feel refreshed, and clear out your lymphatic system.

Long (10 minutes or more)

- Mantra (1 minute)
  Find a cozy spot and sit comfortably. Repeat a positive mantra such as, "I am capable and strong."

- Intention setting (1 minute)
  Set a meaningful intention for the day, for example, "I will approach challenges with a positive mindset."

- Journal (2 minutes)
  Write down a few thoughts in your journal. Reflect on your intention and list three goals for the day.

- Movement (2 minutes)
  Engage in a short exercise routine, such as a few yoga stretches or a quick dance to your favorite song to get your blood flowing.

- Music (1 minute)
  Play an uplifting song while you continue your routine. Let the music boost your mood and energy.

- Fun snack (1 minute)
  Prepare a quick and fun snack, like a handful of mixed nuts
  or a small piece of chocolate, to enjoy as you go about your
  morning.

- Crystal roller (1 minute)
  Use your cold crystal roller (stored in the fridge) on your
  face, taking a moment to enjoy the calming sensation, feel
  refreshed, and clear out your lymphatic system.

- Cozy spot relaxation (1 minute)
  Return to your cozy spot, take a deep breath, and spend a
  final moment visualizing a successful and fulfilling day ahead.

These routines can also be adapted to help you unwind, reflect on your
day, and prepare your mind and body for a restful night's sleep as you
prepare for bed.

Evening Routine

Prepare physically for bed (putting on pajamas, brushing teeth,
washing face) before or after routine.

Short (5 minutes or fewer)

- Mantra (1 minute)
  Find a cozy spot, such as a comfortable chair or a corner with
  soft cushions.

- Sit quietly and repeat a calming mantra like, "I release the
  day's stress and embrace peace."

- Intention setting (1 minute)
  While in your cozy spot, set an intention for the night, such as, "My intention is to rest and rejuvenate."

- Journal (1 minute)
  Take out your journal and quickly jot down three things you're grateful for that happened during the day.

- Movement (1 minute)
  Do a gentle stretch or a brief yoga pose to relax your muscles and release any tension.

- Crystal roller (1 minute)
  Use your cold crystal roller on your face, enjoying the calming and cooling effect as you wind down.

Long (10 minutes or more)

- Mantra (1 minute)
  Find a cozy spot and sit comfortably. Repeat a soothing mantra such as, "I am grateful for today and look forward to tomorrow."

- Intention setting (1 minute)
  Set a restful intention for the night like, "I will sleep deeply and wake up refreshed."

- Journal (2 minutes)
  Reflect on your day by writing in your journal. Write down three things you're grateful for and any thoughts or events you'd like to remember.

- Movement (2 minutes)
  Engage in a gentle exercise routine, such as a few calming yoga stretches or a short walk to help your body relax.

- Music (1 minute)
  Play a calming song or some soft instrumental music to create a peaceful atmosphere.

- Fun snack (1 minute)
  Enjoy a light and comforting snack, such as a handful of popcorn or a granola bar to help you unwind.

- Crystal roller (1 minute)
  Use your cold crystal roller on your face, taking a moment to relax and enjoy the soothing sensation.

- Cozy spot relaxation (1 minute)
  Return to your cozy spot, take a deep breath, and spend a final moment visualizing a peaceful and restorative night's sleep.

MomSquad Secret

Love yourself through the hardest days. You deserve a lot of grace. No one else knows what it's like to parent your kids in this current year. —Mary E.

Section 3

Let Yourself BLOOM

"And the day came when the risk to remain tight in a bud was more painful than the risk it took to blossom."[31]

— **Elizabeth Appell**

[31] Elizabeth Appell as Lacy Bennett, inspirational header on a flier for the adult education program at John F. Kennedy University, Orinda, California, 1979 (verified here https://adventuresinjournalism.substack.com/p/whose-line-is-it-anyway and on Wikiquote https://en.wikiquote.org/wiki/Ana%C3%AFs_Nin).

NINE
OVERCOMING OBSTACLES:
Removing Boulders

(Your Healing Journey)

"Earth laughs in flowers."[32]

– Ralph Waldo Emerson

---

[32] Ralph Waldo Emerson, "Hamatreya," published in John Bartlett, *Bartlett's Familiar Quotes*, 10th ed. (New York City: Little Brown and Co., 1917).

You might **want** to grow flowers, but there are large boulders—obstacles—in the way of your garden being ready for planting. The amount and size of these obstacles is uniquely personal. Each one of us has boulders that limit our growth and our expression. Depending on the season of life that we are in, our boulders will shift and change with us. But a boulder is always a boulder no matter what shape or size it is. They are obstacles holding us back from living our greatest and most fulfilling lives.

One boulder in my life prior to fully blooming was healing my thoughts toward sexuality. This problem didn't manifest when I was younger, but lack of experience and unhealthy expectations regarding sex were completely exposed in the first few years of my marriage. I was taught that sex was only for marriage and that it was used to create life. While there were hints that sex could be pleasurable—whether those hints came from friends, family, or media—it was considered a "naughty" topic and wasn't something normal to talk about in everyday conversation. How I was raised helped me to remain sexually pure in my younger years, but lack of the proper balance in education about sex made sexual encounters unpleasurable and awkward well into my marriage. I felt as though a part of me was missing and after asking for advice from several people and resources, I found it hard to find the right "answer."

There's not always "an answer," at least not in a clear cut, one-size-fits-all way to consciously impart wisdom. After all, sex often occurs within a marriage. It is not only a way to have children but also a means to claim your pleasure.

As I researched and decided to understand my relationship to sexual intimacy, I found that I could claim my power over my sexual pleasure. Ever since this part of me was awakened, I feel complete. It was an area of my life that needed healing. I can understand and appreciate, to a point, the boundaries and cautions I was raised to follow—the "purity culture." However, I wonder if there could have been a better way in my past to instill both self–virtue and exploration. Claiming one of my most important identity flowers has impacted my level of joy, creation, and intimacy in life. It has nourished me AND my marriage.

Don't wait for healing like I did. We have within us the ability to heal. It's time to take back our power. Claim your pleasure. Are there areas in your life that need healing? Find someone to talk to about it. Acquire the help and resources. Maybe you've already grown the identity flower of sexuality and you want to cultivate other flowers, or maybe it's not the right growing season for it in your life. What flowers **do** you want in your bouquet? What boulders, or obstacles, need to be overcome before planting those flowers?

Perhaps you're invited on a girl's trip and you have a nursing baby. One of your friends says, "Just get a babysitter!" In your head, you calculate all of the obstacles involved in that "just."

"Just" find someone you trust who is also available to watch the baby for the entirety of the trip.

"Just" have the resources to pay for childcare.

"Just" hope that your baby will take a bottle.

"Just" pump breast milk in advance for storage and then pump while you're away.

"Just" pack all of the necessary clothing and items for the baby.

"Just" prepare for numerous eventualities.

"Just" ensure the caregiver has access to important medical information about the baby, including emergency contacts, healthcare provider details, and any specific health needs or medications.

"Just" plan travel logistics, including transportation and accommodation of the car seat.

"Just" push away all thoughts of feeling guilty or anxious about leaving your baby.

"Just" be ready for messes when you get home.

Not to mention all of the tasks, packing, and planning included for YOU to go on the trip.

Sometimes, it's emotionally easier, socially easier, physically easier, and monetarily easier to stay home. If these obstacles are too daunting—or life-draining—to overcome, it probably isn't the ideal planting season to participate in this type of healing and soul-care. It won't always be this way; you can participate in the future. If these obstacles do seem surmountable—or life-giving—say yes to the trip and yes to the holistic healing experience of addressing emotional, social, and psychological needs while fostering a sense of joy, rejuvenation, and connection.

Is there an area of healing you can identify that has fewer obstacles to overcome? After I had my third child, I was told during my six-week checkup that I had diastasis recti—separation of the abs. The nurse told me to purchase a course on YouTube to heal it and that only the worst cases resulted in surgery. At the time, I was too afraid to spend even a minor amount on an online course. I had intense, breathtaking pain every so often after strenuous, not-recommended exercise (biking uphill with a trailer, pushing a wagon with three children, etc.) I talked to a few friends who worked with women to heal diastasis recti and researched online treatment but was never very consistent in working to heal it personally. Two years later, I was finally willing to spend the time, energy, and money on working to heal it with a pelvic floor physical therapist, but it took time to work through the barriers that were keeping me from taking the path to heal.

Perhaps there's a hobby you haven't engaged in for a while. Name the obstacles in working back up to incorporating that hobby back into your life. Are the obstacles fewer than the steps involved in taking a girl's trip or going to physical therapy? Let's find an area for you, big or small, that can be a win for you to build from.

MomSquad Secrets

Do one thing each day that is more permanent (hang a picture, create a work of art, leave a legacy) because your circumstances certainly change daily! —Amanda

"Fringe hours are those little pockets of time throughout the day that often go underutilized or wasted altogether. They're the moments spent waiting in line, commuting, or even those few minutes before bed. By identifying and prioritizing these moments, you can reclaim valuable time to invest in yourself and pursue your passions. . . . Every woman needs time to refuel, pursue passions, and thrive. Finding these moments is the key to living the life you love."[33] —Jessica N. Turner

Areas of healing or personality I want to incorporate:

_____

_____

_____

_____

Obstacles (Boulders) to overcome prior to execution:

_____

_____

_____

_____

There will be flowers that remain growing in your garden and other flowers you want to cut and place in a curated bouquet. You get to choose what you cultivate and harvest and what you don't.

Witnessing your personal boulders is the first step toward clearing them out and making room for your identity flowers to bloom. It's essential to recognize these obstacles not as insurmountable barriers but as challenges you can address and overcome. Just as a gardener meticulously removes rocks from the soil to prepare for planting, you

---

[33] Jessica N. Turner, *The Fringe Hours: Making Time for You,* (Grand Rapids: Revell, 2015).

must be willing to confront and work through the issues holding you back. This process might be daunting, but it is necessary for growth and transformation.

Think about the boulders in your life that are limiting your potential. They may come in various forms, such as deep-seated fears, societal expectations, or past experiences that continue to influence your present. By identifying and addressing these obstacles, you can begin to clear the path for your true self to emerge. Whether it's healing your thoughts toward sexuality, managing the challenges of motherhood, or finding time for self-development, each step you take to remove these boulders brings you closer to a more fulfilling and authentic life.

Remember, the process of growth is continuous and ever-evolving. You don't have to tackle every boulder at once. Start with the ones you can manage now and gradually work your way through the others. As you do, you will find that your capacity to handle larger obstacles increases. Each small victory builds confidence and resilience, empowering you to take on more significant challenges in the future. Embrace the journey of self-discovery and growth, knowing that every effort you make contributes to a more vibrant and enriched life.

Your garden is waiting to bloom to its full potential and beauty. By acknowledging and removing the boulders in your way, you open up space for your dreams and aspirations to flourish. Life will always present obstacles, but it's how you choose to address and overcome them that defines your path. Be brave, be persistent, and be willing to invest in yourself. The journey might be challenging, but the rewards of living a life true to your values and passions are immeasurable. Take the first step today, and watch as your garden of possibilities begins to thrive.

Bloom Tip:

> Make your WHY big enough. Frame it, if desired. Update it if and when it changes.

My WHY:

_____

_____

_____

_____

Examples:

Working on myself and my goals boosts my mental health and helps me handle parenting stress better.

Empowered mothers create empowered children.

Growing personally makes me more confident and helps me show my kids how to keep learning and growing.

TEN
THE GARDENER:
Community

(The People Who Help
Us in Our Garden)

"Quite often we change jobs, friends, and spouses
instead of ourselves."[34]

—Akbarali H. Jetha

---

[34] Akbarali H. Jetha, *Reflections: Combined Edition*, Self-published, 1994.

We may all have boulders that stand in the way of our blooming, but we don't have to face these obstacles alone. Community plays an essential role in helping us fully bloom. Throughout my life I've experienced the profound impact of community through friends, family, and even neighbors. My journey is a testament to the power of connection, faith, and intention in overcoming life's boulders and achieving personal growth.

I moved to a new state when I was in fourth grade. It took me about a month to adjust to the change. I prayed for a friend and I was given one almost immediately after praying. In middle school, all the students seemed to stay grouped together by the elementary school they attended. Since I didn't have a large friend base in this still new-to-me state, I prayed for some friends. Again, I was given new friends. In junior high, I prayed for another friend and I met a girl who had also grown up in another state. High school was a rough time for me. My school split after my first year and I didn't have anyone to eat lunch with for a long time. Every night I would play this song and it definitely got me through that rough patch.

> *Here's a little song to help you get along.*
> *It will see you through when you're feeling blue.*
> *And though it's not profound, when you're feeling down, so down,*
> *Sing this little tune, and you'll feel better soon.*
>
> *You're not alone,*
> *Even when you're feeling on your own.*
> *You are loved in ways that can't be shown;*

Your needs are known;
You're not alone.

Ane when you cry,
You're just letting go of heartache deep inside.
So tomorrow there'll be sunshine and sky –
And love close by;
You're not alone.

And we know that it's not easy,
But we know that it won't last.
'Cause One who loves you more than me
Is sending blessings fast.

You're not alone,
Say it one more time.
"I'm not alone."
And even when it's hard to find the words,
Our prayers are heard.
We're not alone,
You're not alone.[35]

I prayed for a friend and, just as the previous times, I was given a friend with whom to eat lunch. Through prayer, I've witnessed blessings unfold in the form of meaningful friendships, each one

---

[35] *You're Not Alone*, written and recorded by Michael McLean, Shining Star Music, 1982, music and lyrics printed in *The New Era*, January 1, 1984, https://www.churchofjesuschrist.org/media/music/songs/youre-not-alone?lang=eng.

evidence of divine guidance and answered prayers. By setting clear intentions and believing in the power of God, I've cultivated a mindset that attracts positive experiences into my life. Actively pursuing opportunities to connect with others has not only fulfilled my desire for companionship but also honed my social skills and expanded my perspective. These experiences reinforce the belief that I play an active role in shaping my reality through faith, action, and personal growth, reminding me to continue aligning my intentions with the universe's abundant blessings.

We are not alone. We have the tools within us to create a community. We are wired for connection. We are not meant to parent in isolation.

MomSquad Secret

You don't have to be your child(ren)'s playmate. Invite your child(ren) to participate in what you're currently doing: laundry, cooking, cleaning, etc. Not only will this allow you to get the things done you need to, it will also instill valuable life skills and the value of hard work in your child(ren).

When you do want to dedicate time specifically toward playing with your child(ren), invite them into play that you specifically enjoy. —Ali

Remember what it was like to be their age. —Amber

Growing up, perhaps you were in a family like mine—we would rush to clean the house and make it "presentable" when we found out a guest was coming over. We would shove clothes and blankets into closets, bury the paper piles in a cupboard, and clear off the counters. We would apologize for what little messes remained and act so embarrassed that it appeared unkempt.

> *She had blue skin,*
> *And so did he.*
> *He kept it hid*
> *And so did she.*
> *They searched for blue*
> *Their whole life through,*
> *Then passed right by—*
> *And never knew.*[36]
> **—Shel Silverstein**

When we hide part of ourselves, we sacrifice potential connections and bonding experiences that could have been forged with that part of us. We end up forming inauthentic relationships based on the pretenses we show.

After three years of having my podcast, I felt I had hit a wall in building my audience. All of my friends and family knew about it, and I didn't have much traction in moving past that.

------

[36] Shel Silverstein, "Masks," *Every Thing on It*, (New York City: HarperCollins, 2011).

I had just moved to a new neighborhood and was curious about the small businesses around me. I decided to compile a directory of them for my personal use as a way to support local businesses. People began asking me for this resource and we began having business networking lunches.

This has grown my podcast more than anything else I've tried. More than that, I'm now surrounded by new friends, entrepreneurs, and creators. I'm living in a higher frequency energy vibration and it's spreading.

I love to celebrate new entrepreneurs, especially women. In collaboration with my friend Sara, we have thrown several business "baby" showers. I was at a baby shower last year where the theme was Baby in Bloom. This was the first time the floral motifs really resonated with me. I made a slight alteration in the name and our business showers have become Business in Bloom.

It is incredible to breathe new life into these women's businesses, to stand by them and be there as their businesses bloom. Just as plants need sunlight to survive, we need community. As we light each other up in our pursuits to become, we are imparting that life-giving sunshine that will cause massive growth over time.

My husband has stood by me through every iteration of myself. Many times, I've come home and it's as if he says, "You brought home a whale? Well, that's inconvenient. I'd better start building an aquarium!" He is so very supportive. Find the people that rally around and support you. It may not be within your family. Go to the people that cheer you on, acknowledge your wins, and cry with you during your losses.

> "Shared joy is double joy; shared sorrow is half a
> sorrow."
> **—Swedish Proverb**

We need to have a place to go to celebrate with one another and a place to lessen our suffering. It is essential to have someone with whom to share the good stuff and the hard stuff.

While it's true that we are ultimately responsible for meeting our own needs and understanding ourselves, having a spouse, partner, or community can enrich our lives in various ways. Companionship, emotional support, shared experiences, and mutual growth are just a few benefits of healthy relationships. While they may not fully replace our own self-reliance, they can complement it and add depth and richness to our lives. Additionally, having supportive partners or friends can enhance our overall well-being and contribute to a sense of belonging and connection in the world.

My husband, Jared, and I had been married six months when I walked into our spare bedroom and observed what a mess it had become. Beneath the computer desk were totes full of items from before we were married. There was a piano keyboard with camping gear underneath. One corner held wedding decorations with gifts sprawled about. Also in the room was my husband's puzzle table. By "table" I mean two cases of plastic water bottles stacked on one another with a thin sheet of plywood on top; he was currently in the middle of a

1000-piece puzzle. The room also held food storage, clothes, and seasonal decor. It was definitely a catch-all room.

I decided to start organizing it and began rearranging items. I grabbed a sleeping bag to move it to the top shelf of the closet. Almost as if in slow motion, the sleeping bag fell out of my hands and crashed onto the puzzle table. Pieces went *everywhere*, cascading down to the floor. With horror, I realized the ramifications of what I had done.

Jared was home at the time and ran into the room to see if I was okay. Through sobs I told him what had happened. He pulled me into a hug, consoling *me* for ruining *his* puzzle. He reassured me that it was okay and that puzzles come that way. They are meant to be put back together. Now he would get to do it again!

We are like puzzles. We are meant to come apart, not remain complete. Just because you're not complete doesn't mean you're not whole. **You alone are entirely whole, just as you are.** You have all the ingredients for success. God sees all the pieces put together.

MomSquad Secret

I have never liked my thighs. I feel they are too big, too hairy, too ugly. I am working to accept them.

In the past I was self-conscious about how low my voice is. Hearing my voice podcasting has helped that in some regards. I expressed this dislike to my husband a while ago. He said if my voice was any higher pitched, it would grate on his ears! Little did I know that my voice was within his ideal hearing range. You don't have to change something in order to accept it.

Life looks so different on Instagram, even though I know logically that what's shown is the highlight reel. One mom posts a picturesque day at the park, another shares an outing to a museum, still another talks about the sweet bond she's formed because of breastfeeding her newborn.

People reinforce these idealistic fantasies: A husband who is tall, dark, and handsome? How dreamy! Children two years apart? How perfect. A boy and a girl? How perfect. An even number of children? How perfect—now they each have a buddy. There are so many societal expectations for how life should look. "You're such a good mom!"

Before we can ever accept what is, we have to process and grieve what we thought it could be. Just as I had a hope for the mom I thought I wanted to have, I had to let go of my agenda first to truly be at peace with where I am.

Just as I found friends through prayer and intention, you, too, can call in the right community for your growth. Setting clear intentions and asking for support from a higher power can align you with the people who will help you flourish. Remember, it's not just about asking; it's about being open and receptive to the connections that come your way. By embracing the power of prayer and intention, you can create a supportive network that nurtures your personal growth and helps you overcome the boulders in your path.

Prayer and intention are powerful tools that can help us attract the right people into our lives. When we pray for guidance and support, we are not just asking for divine intervention but also setting our minds to recognize and embrace opportunities for connection. It's about aligning our desires with our actions, ensuring that we are actively seeking out and nurturing the relationships that will help us grow.

Your community is out there waiting to be discovered. By being intentional and proactive in your approach, you can build a network of like-minded individuals who will support and uplift you. These connections will provide the encouragement and strength needed to navigate life's challenges and celebrate its joys. Don't underestimate the power of reaching out, both through prayer and direct action, to create the community you need.

Embrace the journey of building your community with an open heart and a willing spirit. Understand that each person you connect with is a piece of your growth puzzle. Together, you can create a vibrant, supportive environment that fosters both individual and collective blossoming. Let your intentions guide you, and trust that the right people will come into your life at the right time to help you to bloom in ways you never imagined possible.

MomSquad Secret

She may look like a perfect mom but she loses it too, sometimes. —Sarah H.

Bloom Tip:

Learn to laugh throughout. Sometimes all we need is some comedic relief. —Shannon

ELEVEN
THE WHOLE BOUQUET:

Curating

(Ongoing Care)

"What's left for us to prize? I think it's this: to do (and not do) what we were designed for. That's the goal of all trades, all arts, and what each of them aims at: that the thing they create should do what it was designed to do."[37]

—Marcus Aurelius

---

[37] Marcus Aurelius, *Meditations: Sixth Book*, XV, available on Project Gutenberg, https://www.gutenberg.org/cache/epub/2680/pg2680-images.html#link2H_4_0128 (eBook released 2001), quoted material translated into modern language by Gregory Hays, *Meditations: A New Translation*, (New York City: Modern Library, 2003).

Do you find that you want to wait for the perfect time, situation, and opportunity to showcase your strengths and talents? I find that most women want to have everything perfect before they begin.

But did you know that the optimal time to harvest flowers is not when they're fully open? Rather, it is recommended to cut them when the bud is closed and has not yet unfolded. When done this way, bouquets can be admired for a much longer period of time. It can feel counterintuitive or even painful to pluck a flower from the ground before it has bloomed, but doing so will yield more enjoyment as a result. Similarly, you may feel you are not qualified, ready, or worthy to prepare your bouquet. However, embracing this approach allows you to enjoy the beauty of your bouquet for a longer time and teaches you that the right timing is essential for continued growth and fulfillment.

Now is the perfect time to nourish your identity, especially if you have young children. These formative years are when they need you the most, making it crucial for you to maintain a strong sense of self. By investing in your personal growth and nurturing your passions, you not only model resilience and self-love for your children but also equip yourself with the inner strength you need to navigate the demands of motherhood. Embracing and enriching your identity now will provide a solid foundation that will carry you through these challenging yet rewarding times, ensuring you remain a whole, fulfilled individual for yourself and your family. The care you give yourself now will set a precedent of care throughout motherhood.

When you've harvested your flowers, it's time to arrange your bouquet. Your core values have bloomed and are skillfully placed within the bouquet. Motherhood does not feel as all-consuming anymore because it is simply one of the identity flowers—one of the many roles you hold. Every day, you make sure that your bouquet has a reservoir of water and you continue to water your garden and greenhouses where still other attributes are growing. You routinely test the soil so that you know when it's missing key nutrients. When winter comes, you acknowledge its importance in the germination process. You see scarification periods as opportunities for new growth. Even though pinching is a painful process, you know it will yield more flowers in the long run. You live in your season and recognize that there are optimal times for growth and that each period is not without its obstacles. At harvest time, you willingly pick the closed flowers because you know doing so will allow for a longer window of being in bloom. The gardener is on site and is instrumental in supporting the process of growth. You are not ashamed of your bouquet nor do you feel guilty about the number of flowers present. You tend to your flowers and know that you are equally as deserving of being nurtured and loved as a child is deserving of being nurtured and loved.

Of course, "bloom where you're planted"[38] (as a mother or in your current role) but also, create and curate your own garden! Just because you were placed in a set of circumstances doesn't necessarily mean you need to remain there. Take full ownership of your potential.

---

[38] Saint Francis de Sales, French priest of late 16th and early 17th centuries. Original quote: "Bloom in the garden where [God] has planted [you]."

Embody this version of you because *it is* you. Perhaps it's a future version, an iteration you're working toward, but it's you. Your bouquet is curated with intention. It's a beautiful culmination of all of you in your full identity and power. We love each bouquet and each bouquet is whole. Your bouquet is a culmination of who you are as your most empowered self.

You get to display this version for all to admire and benefit from visually. The fragrance is potent and divine. Each flower complements another and the bouquet wouldn't be as beautiful without all the variety.

When cultivating gardens, there are so many ways to go about it. There are lovely flower gardens, there are eye-catching areas of wildflower growth, and there are a myriad of combinations in between. Many people decide what they want their landscape to look like based on how much energy they're willing to put in or pay to maintain it. I have given you small, actionable ways to nurture your garden. Get ready to cultivate a garden that truly reflects your core values and dreams.

Can your identity be put into words, or is it something bigger than that? For many, identity is a blend of experiences, beliefs, relationships, and personal growth. It encompasses not just who you are in the present but also your past and your potential future. While words can capture aspects of identity, the full essence of who you are often transcends simple descriptions. We're going to articulate at least the elements of identity we've worked on throughout this book.

What's your garden going to look like?

Soil represents your strengths. Write down the strengths you found and the new title you gave yourself.

_____

_____

_____

_____

_____

Seeds represent core values. What are your 3–5 core values? Can you remember what you wrote down? Work to KNOW these core values.

_____

_____

_____

_____

Soul-care is how you tend to your garden. What is one thing you can do each day that will help nourish you and care for you?

_____

_____

_____

_____

Goals are also the seeds you plant in your garden. What goals are you planting?

_____

_____

_____

_____

_____

_____

Greenhouses help you contain and nurture your identity flowers/goals. How are you taking care of your goals?

_____

_____

_____

_____

_____

Fertilizer represents balance. Are there areas in your life that need more balance? What does that look like?

_____

_____

_____

_____

_____

_____

Adversity is often a catalyst for growth. What adversity are you facing right now?

_____

_____

_____

_____

_____

_____

Weeds are inevitable. And for optimal growth, they must be pulled. How are you going to pull the weeds in your life?

_____

_____

_____

_____

_____

Removing boulders provides more space. How much space do you want in your garden? Do you want margins in your day, or do you want it to be packed full? What boulders do you need to remove or overcome?

_____

_____

_____

_____

Community helps gardens flourish. What does your community look like and do you want more, new, or different communities in your life?

_____

_____

_____

_____

_____

_____

Maintaining is also part of the deal. When you buy an item, you now have another item to maintain. Some items require more maintenance than others. You wouldn't buy a toothbrush, brush your teeth once, and then call it good for the rest of your life.

Similarly, your identity is worth maintaining. I know that maintaining takes bandwidth. But I know it is worth it. Your garden is a lot more spacious after the work you've done to curate it. Make it sustainable for the long-term, knowing that different seasons require different care tactics. Seasons of personal wintering will call for more of a sacred retreat. Seasons of growth in seemingly scorching heat will demand additional watering and nutrients. There will be times to sit and relax in your garden, and other times that will need consistent work to remove weeds. During my current season, motherhood is my biggest crop, thus it takes up more space than it might in other seasons. I am giving care and attention to the areas that are needed, and you can too.

Pruning is important because gardens and flowers become overgrown without it. If left alone, the flowers in a garden will get choked out by the weeds, their beauty drowned out by lack of attention. Alternatively, if a garden is maintained, it will be full of beauty and vitality, bringing joy and fragrance to the world. A garden that is pruned and maintained thrives.

So, as you embark on this journey of tending to your unique garden, remember that perfection is not the goal. Embrace the beauty of each stage, from planting seeds to nurturing blooms. Celebrate the vibrant colors and diverse fragrances that each flower brings to your bouquet. Know that your strengths, values, and goals are all part of this intricate, beautiful arrangement. By caring for your garden with intention, you honor every aspect of your identity and allow yourself to flourish. Your bouquet, in all its glory, is a testament to your growth, resilience, and the boundless potential within you. Let it be a source of inspiration, both for yourself and for those who have the privilege of witnessing your bloom. Keep tending, keep growing, and know that your garden is a living, breathing masterpiece of your empowered self.

Bloom Tip:

> "What you get by achieving your goals is not as important as what you become by achieving your goals."[39] —Zig Ziglar

Take a moment to reflect on a recent goal you've achieved. Write down the skills, qualities, or new perspectives you gained in the

---

[39] Zig Ziglar, qtd. by Lilly Walters, *Secrets of Superstar Speakers: Wisdom from the Greatest Motivators of Our Time*, (New York City: McGraw-Hill, 2000), 96.

process. Identify one of these new strengths and find a way to apply it to your current or future goals. This practice not only reinforces your growth but also helps you stay focused on personal development rather than just the end results.

Goal I've achieved in the past six months or fewer:

_____

_____

_____

_____

Skills, qualities, or new perspectives I've gained:

_____

_____

_____

_____

Circle one aspect you'd like to apply to a future goal.

TWELVE
IN FULL BLOOM:
Unfolding

(Full Heart Send)

"The greatest gift I could give to you is if you could see yourself the way I do."[40]

—**Caption added to painting**
"Christ and Young Women"

---

[40] Del Parson, "Christ and Young Women," release date unknown, available at Deseret Book, https://www.deseretbook.com/product/P4530465.html.

In your vibrant, diverse garden, each flower represents a unique aspect of your identity. Some flowers are colorful and fully bloomed, while others are still growing, symbolizing different strengths, experiences, and facets of who you are. In the midst of this garden, there's a clay flower pot that appears unremarkable at first glance. However, as time passes and the elements wear away the clay, a golden gleam begins to shine through. Curious gardeners gently remove the remaining clay, revealing a pot made of pure gold.

This golden flower pot represents the hidden potential and intrinsic worth within each of us. Just as the garden is filled with different flowers, our identities are multi-faceted and beautiful. The discovery of the golden pot among the flowers shows that even parts of ourselves we might initially overlook or undervalue hold immense beauty and worth.

Mama, I get it. The exhaustion, the constant demands, and the emotional ups and downs can feel overwhelming. I've been there, and I know how tough it can be.

I heard how you nursed, pumped, diapered, cleaned, put the baby down, and then did it all over again. You were so sleep-deprived, and your husband wouldn't even help by washing the bottles. You felt alone, with no one in your corner. No one could do it for you, and no one seemed to understand. You did it, but it was hard, and you got tired of trite responses. You needed to be rescued, not just helped. When you're in survival mode, you can't rescue yourself.

I understand because you've shared moments with me—the time when you were carrying laundry, stepped on Legos, and everything fell apart.

All of that folded laundry came tumbling down and the thought, *I'm drowning* echoed in your mind, over and over again.

I see you crying, trying to hold it together and keep face for your children. You wonder how you have all of this time with children yet no time for yourself. You're bossed around, taken for granted, and used.

Amid the chaos of wiping three bums in twenty minutes and unexpectedly finding poop on your shirt, it was easy to overlook the small joys. But woven into these hectic moments are reminders of the good things: the warmth of holding a chubby baby's hand, the sweet smell of a newborn, the comforting sound of their breath as they sleep on your chest, and the contagious giggles that light up your day. Even during naptime, when you find yourself missing them, these fleeting yet precious moments stand out, reminding you of the deep joys of parenthood.

I would like to acknowledge you for the hard work and dedication you put into caring for your children and managing daily responsibilities. I recognize that motherhood comes with a range of emotions and challenges, and your range of emotions is valid. As cliché as it sounds, you ARE doing a great job. I know you are because you're reading this book. You are making huge sacrifices, whether it's sleep, personal time, or career aspirations, to prioritize your children. I am celebrating your achievements, big and small, including milestones in parenting and personal accomplishments outside of motherhood. I am here for you. I respect your identity beyond motherhood. You have amazing interests, passions, and goals. I support your efforts to take time for soul-care and personal well-being. I commend you for navigating the complexities of your experiences and challenges. I am grateful for your role in shaping families and communities.

Amid the challenges and chaos of motherhood, remember that there are moments of profound joy and fulfillment waiting to be cherished. You are not alone on this journey; countless mothers stand with you, each navigating their own unique garden path. Take a moment to honor your incredible strength and resilience, for you are capable of more than you may realize. Embrace the small joys and milestones, the giggles, the first steps, the quiet moments of connection. These are the treasures that make the journey worthwhile.

It's essential to prioritize soul-care and your own well-being. A nourished and balanced self is the foundation upon which you build your family's happiness. You are not just raising children; you are shaping lives, instilling values, and making a difference every single day.

Thank you for sharing this journey with me. Your openness, your willingness to grow, and your dedication to both your children and yourself are truly inspiring. Together, we navigate the complexities of motherhood, celebrating the highs and supporting each other through the lows. We are a community, a sisterhood bound by love and shared experience.

Here's to embracing the journey with courage, love, and an unwavering spirit. Trust in your instincts, lean on your support systems, and never forget that you are enough. You've got this. And as we continue this beautiful, messy, and rewarding journey, let's do so with hearts full of hope and determination. Here's to you, to us, and to the incredible adventure of motherhood. You've got this.

MomSquad Secrets

"We fancy that God can only manage His world by big battalions . . . when all the while He is doing it by beautiful babies. . . . When a wrong wants righting, or a work wants doing, or a truth wants preaching, or a continent wants opening, God sends a baby into the world to do it. That is why, long, long ago, a babe was born at Bethlehem."[41]—F. W. Boreham (quoted by Sara K.)

The love of a mother is one of the most powerful forces in the world. What mothers endure for their children is immeasurable. —Irene

Bloom Tip:

Mama, I know you can do this. I know you think you can't add more, but I promise if you *let yourself bloom*, your overwhelm will dissipate. Your joy will expand.

---

[41] F.W. Boreham, *Mountains in the Mist: Some Australian Reveries*, (New York: Abingdon, 1919).

ACKNOWLEDGMENTS

This book would not be what it is without the many people who helped along the way. I am immensely grateful for each one of you.

THE WRITING PROCESS

A Journal Entry

A garden is curated. You don't always see the work that goes into it. I pulled a lot of weeds to get to this point. Conveying an experience through written words is tricky, but I will write it as I remember it.

Keira Brinton, founder of JOA publishing, offers author adventures as a way to write your book. She takes you to a tailored location and you write your book in a week. Yes, *one week.*

On Monday, the very first morning of our adventure, we did a lot of preparation. We had a lengthy breathwork session which felt like an exfoliation of my insides. We then blessed our bodies (all of our chakras), and pulled cards from "The Divine Feminine Oracle" deck.

We spent a lot of time meditating, praying, and just being. The whole week was one of the most spiritual experiences of my life; we wrote the messages God wanted us to write. My publisher always says, "The precision of the ask is the magnet to the result." The more we can get specific about what answer we're seeking, the clearer our response will be to guide our words.

I did get a bit antsy toward the end of the preparation phase—I was anxious to get writing! Wasn't that why we were there?! In retrospect, I am so grateful for the ways it cleansed me to write, opened up my mind, and healed my nervous system. We wrote for the afternoon and then stopped for dinner. During dinner we each talked about the words that came through for us and our biggest takeaways for the day.

After dinner, we went for a walk on the loop around our AirBnb. Keira filmed us stating that we were now authors. I was very timid as I made my video, especially with the others watching. They cheered just as loudly for me nonetheless. It was fabulous to be supported by a community (two other writers, my publisher, and my editor). Before bed, Keira used her drum to clear the energy and we pulled more cards. The card that was pulled for me was Kali.

An excerpt from her description:

> "Kali embodies the ultimate wake-up call to get us aligned as soon as possible with what we have come here to do . . ."[42]

I woke up on Tuesday a newer, bolder version of myself, ready to write without fear of judgment!

The remainder of the week followed the pattern of the first day, just in a smaller sense. We began each day at 9:00 a.m. (you could wake up and write earlier if you wanted, which I did a couple of the days), stopped for an hour lunch, and finished up around 6:00 p.m. for

---

[42] Meggan Watterson, *The Divine Feminine Oracle Guidebook*, (Carlsbad: Hay House, 2018).

dinner. Tuesday morning, we wrote in the actual Muir Woods. A park ranger walked by me as I typed on my laptop and said, "So, this is your office today too, eh?"

The Muir Woods are right above San Francisco and they are filled with huge, incredible trees! I can't even convey their magnitude. They have been there for centuries! But there are also the most magnificent clovers on the ground. When I visited the national park, I took pictures of the clovers as well as the trees. This is like motherhood in many ways: it is possible to find more joy in motherhood if we change our focus to include both the big and the small tender moments.

In the Muir Woods, where I am writing this book, there are the most incredible trees. They grow in clusters; they share a base! One tree fell and branches are still growing upward out of it. Trees defy gravity. They are not held down, held back, by the heaviness. They reach for the light. They are in community. This shows that roots are not the only source of strength. We can rely on the people around us, look upward, while also depending on the strength within.

As we were making our way out of the Muir Woods, Keira had us each select a tree, touch it, and listen to its wisdom. A synopsis of what we each "heard":

The Wisdom of the Trees

Keira: "Okay, so I put my hand on the tree and I started to worry about an ant crawling on it because there were just so many ants and I was just paranoid. And so the message was, stop worrying if the ant is going to crawl on your hand. If it does, you'll deal with it. Stop worrying about things that haven't happened. If they do, you will deal with them. As a problem arises, you always find the solution. Always. Trust. I never worried about how tall I would get. I just grew."

Trisha: "My book is a lot on motherhood. I talk a lot about the pain of bringing forth just one life. Pregnancy was the hardest thing I've ever done. I threw up so much, then, you know, stretch marks and scars, and all of the things that we go through to create life. And so that was on my mind and I walked by and saw this big tree with this trunk that had scars and it was uneven, it had some bumps, it had some lumps. And I was like, hey tree, I feel you sister. You and me, we know each other. Hey lady. So I went up to her and I just put my hands on this tree and I'm not even joking you, I heard, 'Your scars are your beauty for they signify life, pain, and triumph.' And what she had been through, you could see it. And it was like the honor that you have for like fire marks and scars and growth. And I was like, here we are thinking that we need to look twelve forever."

Me: I was inspired by the trees that had collapsed. There were many that had fallen over and were still growing in new ways; they had branches growing vertical even though the trunk was horizontal. And so this one particular tree, it looked just like a log, pretty much, it had moss and flowers and other things growing on it. And the words that came to me were: *roots aren't the only source of strength.*

Brooke: "My tree, I said to it, 'Tree, you've seen so much. I can't imagine how you've even seen.' And the tree said, 'I haven't seen it; I've experienced it. I felt it. It is part of me. And so many things have tried to take me down. Fires, parasites, things that cling to me, things that burrow in me for their home. But I grow within the confines of this, against gravity. I grow in compression of these things and this. . . this is what allows me to be this tall tree you look up to.'"

Mindy: "I was drawn to a tree that had fallen and had an enormous root system that had been unearthed. The roots were gnarled and knotted, and beautiful. I lovingly placed my hands on these roots and asked, 'What message do you have for me? What message can I share with these women I am here with that will help them to write with confidence?' I stood for several minutes, my hands resting on the roots, and listened. And then, the tree spoke directly to my spirit. 'Root into who you *are*. Root into your gifts, your talents, your light. And help them to recognize *their* gifts. Use *your* gifts, your light to help them root into who *they are*.'"

After we left the Muir Woods, we went to a fancy, sit-down restaurant. There were unconventional items on the menu and we deliberated for a time. The waitress came to the table and we asked her for recommendations. She described the soup of the day, listed as an appetizer. She gushed about how it was full of vegetables, including potatoes, carrots, celery, and beets all atop a full, hearty, comforting broth. We were all still deciding on main courses but the soup sounded so great that we ordered two for the table to share. When it arrived, it was clearly only a flat beet soup. Many at the table remarked that it tasted like dirt and was very one-note. We laughed and cried because the waitress had sold it **so well,** so convincingly.

I can relate because I've spent so many years in expectation pain! I had an elaborate vision of what marriage would be. The first month of marriage, I remember making dinner for my husband and me. He commented that the food "wasn't the way his mom made it." Experience after experience eroded my marriage ideals and left me grieving the marriage I thought I would have. I have now reconciled those experiences and have learned to manage my expectations and my brain around circumstances. Just as identity supersedes circumstances, gratitude supersedes circumstances.

On Wednesday I doubled my word count. I wrote about the fewest topics, yet I had the highest word count of the week. I was truly able to dive deep into my book, cathartically writing experiences that have since been removed but helped me immensely in processing my story. That evening, we spent time conversing together in an outdoor hot tub.

On Thursday of this week of my writing adventure, my publisher and I got to talk to the in-house branding agency to design my book cover. We described the message, feel, and audience of the book. While we were talking to the head of the company, her assistant was pulling together an image on the side. Within forty-five minutes, we were able to see what she had come up with based on the information we had shared. I had a general color scheme, had visualized a casual but sophisticated look, and wanted the words "Let Yourself Bloom" written as part of the stems of flowers. Seeing the revealed cover was an incredible experience! Even though it was just a rendering, it felt so real to see my vision as a book.

During the consultation, they had asked if there were specific flowers I wanted to use. I said that I didn't have any particular flowers in mind.

The first rendition has poppies on it. They look beautifully elegant. And I haven't changed a thing since the adventure, the first rendition is the only rendition!

That evening, we went to a spa and we were each treated to a ninety-minute massage. It was so relaxing and healing for my nervous system.

The next day, Friday, I woke up to a message from a spammer on Instagram. I opened the app to block communication and a post on the homepage caught my eye—one with a poppy on the first slide of a carousel. Beneath the poppy was a picture of Taylor Swift and a caption that read "Entering my Swift analysis era: Why would Taylor Swift release a double album at the peak of her over exposure?" (@celestemdavis).

Have you ever heard of The Tall Poppy Syndrome? It refers to our penchant for criticizing, resenting, or ostracizing women when they get too successful. When one poppy grows too tall, we collectively cut her down.

Taylor Swift, more than anyone, is acutely tuned into society's limited tolerance of successful women. The initials of The Tall Poppy Syndrome (TTPS) and her latest double album, *The Tortured Poets Society* (TTPS) can't be a coincidence.

I found it so fitting that the poppy is on the cover of this book. What do we make it mean about us when women are successful? You are allowed to thrive, grow, and succeed. *Let* yourself bloom.

Friday night, we shared portions of our books, verbally, with each other. We hadn't been in each other's books to this level until this point. Before starting to read aloud, Keira shared examples of how we were to share them.

Version #1: "Okay, so like, I'm not sure this is exactly how it'll stay. Remember, it's a first draft. . . . This part's not very good, but here it goes."

Version #2: "'Here's one of my chapters.' And you read it. Done."

Even my publisher was aware of this toxic need to apologize for taking up space.

Saturday was the last day of the author adventure. God sent me the rain. Rain is my absolute favorite weather. I went outside to hear it more clearly and my first thought was to go get my phone to capture its essence. What I heard in my mind was, "Just *be* for a moment." I retracted my steps and stood on the porch to take in the stormy beauty. I then went to take a picture to document the moment. I walked back up to my room with the thought, "I want this as my muse. Where can I go to write in this ambiance?" The answer was, "You don't need to go anywhere. It's all right here." Sure enough, I picked up my laptop and all I needed to do was open the window.

Before rushing to take pictures of a moment or experience in your life, take time to just revel in it. Savor the moment with all of your senses. Soak in the real version before rendering it an artificial memory. As a society, many have lost the ability to simply *be*. There are many things that vie for our attention, especially technologically.

After cleaning up and checking out, we found ourselves with some time before heading to the airport. We decided to soak in the atmosphere at Fisherman's Wharf, savoring the sights and sounds of the bustling waterfront. It was there that my publisher surprised me with a pearl, freshly retrieved from a clam right before our eyes—a symbolic gesture of our journey together. Inspired by the depth of this experience, I made a personal choice to commemorate it with a tattoo. The poppy design, mirroring my book cover, now adorns my skin, serving as a permanent reminder of this transformative adventure and the creative process of writing my book.

Be your own bouquet of flowers and *let yourself bloom.*

Made in the USA
Monee, IL
21 October 2024

68141322R00114